The Popular Song Reader

A Sampler of Well-Known Twentieth-Century Songs

HAWORTH Popular Culture

New, Recent, and Forthcoming Titles
Frank W. Hoffmann and William G. Bailey
Senior Co-Editors

Arts & Entertainment Fads by Frank W. Hoffmann and William G. Bailey

Sports & Recreation Fads by Frank W. Hoffmann and William G. Bailey

Mind & Society Fads by Frank W. Hoffmann and William G. Bailey

Chocolate Fads, Folklore, and Fantasies: 1,000 Chunks of Chocolate Information by Linda Fuller

Fashion and Merchandising Fads by Frank W. Hoffmann and William G. Bailey

The Popular Song Reader: A Sampler of Well-Known Twentieth-Century Songs by William E. Studwell

Rock Music in American Popular Culture: Rock 'n' Roll Resources by B. Lee Cooper and Wayne S. Bailey

The Popular Song Reader

A Sampler of Well-Known Twentieth-Century Songs

William E. Studwell, MSLS, MS

Routledge
Taylor & Francis Group
NEW YORK AND LONDON

First published 1994 by The Haworth Press, Inc.
10 Alice Street, Binghamton, NY 13904-1580

This edition published 2015 by Routledge
711 Third Avenue, New York, NY 10017, USA
2 Park Square, Milton Park, Abingdon, Oxon OX14 4RN

Routledge is an imprint of the Taylor & Francis Group, an informa business

Library of Congress Cataloging-in-Publication Data

Studwell, William E. (William Emmett), 1936-
The popular song reader : a sampler of well-known twentieth-century songs / William E. Studwell.
p. cm.
Essays. Limited to American songs and foreign songs popular in the United States.
Includes index.
Contents: Pops, 1900-1925–Pops, 1926-1952–Pops, 1953 and after–Broadway, 1900-1939–Broadway, 1940 and after–Movies–Television.
ISBN 1-56023-029-0.
1. Popular music–United States–History and criticism.
I. Title.
ML 3477.S78 1993
782.42164'0972–dc20 92-44615
CIP
MN

ISBN 13: 978-1-56023-029-8 (pbk)

CONTENTS

ABOUT THE AUTHOR

William E. Studwell, MSLS, MS, is Professor, University Libraries, at Northern Illinois University in DeKalb. He is the author of reference books on Christmas carols, ballet, and opera, as well as other books on music and several on library science. He has also authored almost 200 articles (over 60 on music) and has made more than 100 appearances in national, regional, and local media. Mr. Studwell is the editor of *Music Reference Services Quarterly* and a member of the American Library Association.

Introduction

The term "pop" pops up regularly in our everyday lives. "Pop" is a slang expression for a less serious style of music, and that is the topic of this book. "Pop" also means father, and if you are one you may remember a lot of songs covered here. "Pop" is what the weasel did, but that little piece is too old to be included in this survey of twentieth-century music. "Pop" is a baseball flying high in the air, but since the usual result is an out, that type of pop doesn't fit with this collection of essays about hits.

"Pop" meaning soda or the sound of a champagne cork implies suitable companions to drink while browsing through this anthology. "Pop" is sometimes connected with "corn" to make "popcorn," which can be consumed with the beverages just mentioned. The frequent touches of humor herewith might also occasionally border on "corn." "Pops" is the name of a serious symphonic orchestra that performs some of the better songs discussed.

All of this playing with a simple three-letter word is a way of suggesting that this volume is a collection of informative material given in a relatively palatable or entertaining environment. Over two hundred essays on twentieth century popular music are presented here, covering not only the two hundred plus featured compositions but hundreds of other songs secondarily or indirectly. Some pieces are mentioned only once, and some come up several times. In all cases the basic data on the song, that is, when and by whom it was created, is given, although in various essays some basic data was skipped because it was included elsewhere.

Only American popular songs, and foreign songs popular in the United States, are part of this survey. Since there are thousands of possible candidates for inclusion, the author's subjective judgments had to put quantitative limits on the number of songs to appear. But whoever picks up this book will quickly discover that there is a wealth of useful and non-useful information included, even if certain songs have for some reason been excluded.

There are seven different sections, each with a somewhat different "personality." The first is "Pops, 1900-1925," covering older style and more traditional songs from Tin Pan Alley and similar sources. The second is "Pops, 1926-1952," covering the creative late twenties, the swing/big band era, and the early post-World War II period. The third is "Pops, 1953 and After," covering the rock era. This section was not as thoroughly covered as the two previous sections for three reasons: (1) it is harder to determine what has become a standard or may be enduring when songs are newer; (2) it is the author's belief that fewer good and lasting songs were written after 1970; and (3) the music of recent decades receives a lot of attention in various media and therefore needs less coverage here. The classic rock years, the 1950s and 1960s, are the general focus of section three.

The fourth section is "Broadway, 1900-1939," covering the songs from Broadway, off-Broadway, and the musical theater in general up to just before the first collaboration of Rodgers and Hammerstein. The fifth section is "Broadway, 1940 and After," featuring the best and most famous stage songs since 1940. The sixth section is "Movies," covering the better-known songs from the film medium. The last section is "Television," covering compositions especially written for use on the tube or most commonly associated with the one-eyed monster.

It could be debated that some of the songs featured in a section technically might not belong there because of dating or origins, but if it seemed that a song was more at home in a certain section, that's where it was placed. In any case, the index should be consulted if data on a certain song is desired since so many compositions discussed do not appear in the headings for the two hundred plus essays. Therefore, this volume serves as both a detailed reference book and as a reader for more continuous perusal.

Overall, this can be described as an effort to comprehensively present a broad spectrum of American popular songs, in their historical and cultural contexts, and also perhaps have a bit of fun. It's a three "E" endeavor–education, enjoyment, and expansion of understanding.

POPS
1900-1925

Alexander's Ragtime Band

At times fate can be cruel. At other times fate can be most kindly and convenient. By sheer accident, the first essay in this book is about the first of the first.

Irving Berlin (1888-1989) was the first among American popular songwriters. A master of a wide range of compositions, including "White Christmas" (number one of twentieth-century carols), "Easter Parade" (number one of secular Easter songs), and "God Bless America" (number one of twentieth-century American patriotic songs), Berlin has no peers. While Stephen Foster may have been the "George Washington" of American songwriters by being the first great popular composer in the United States, Berlin was the "Abraham Lincoln" by freeing the American public from the bonds of mediocre popular music.

Berlin's first big hit was "Alexander's Ragtime Band" (1911). It was intended to be introduced by Berlin at the Friars Club in New York, but things just didn't work out. Subsequent efforts to include "Alexander" in vaudeville shows did not pay off right away, but eventually the song caught on and ultimately became a tremendous success. It really was not written in true ragtime style (jazz with constant syncopation), but instead was a lively march with only a touch of syncopation. Yet it was the most popular ragtime piece ever created and did much to lead the tastes of the public toward the new syncopation fad.

"Alexander" also violated the old adage: "Neither a borrower nor a lender be." Berlin's song was probably inspired by an earlier piece "Alexander, Don't You Love Your Baby No More" and included bugle calls and a snatch from Stephen Foster's "Old Folks at Home" (or "Swanee River"). He even borrowed from himself, reworking the lyrics of his 1910 nonentity "Alexander and His Clarinet" and setting them to one of his previously composed tunes to produce the third and the classic song about Alexander. Later on, the 1911 song was lent to two movies, *Alexander's Ragtime Band* (1938) and *There's No Business Like Show Business* (1954), and played key parts in both.

Fate touched very favorably upon Irving Berlin. He was fortunate to have left his native Russia in his youth and to immigrate to the United States during a heyday of popular music. He was fortunate to have lived 101 years. Most of all, he was fortunate to have a seemingly inexhaustible supply of artistic creativity.

Always

Always is a very long time. Yet Irving Berlin (1888-1989), a perpetual romantic, really did mean forever when he composed the famous 1925 love ballad "Always" in honor of his sweetheart and later wife Ellin. When they married in 1926, Berlin demonstrated the depth of his affection by giving her as a wedding present the legal rights to this highly lucrative song.

"Always" is one of those very familiar standards that seems to sweetly waft in on a variety of occasions from old movies to present-day radio and television programs. It frequently waltzes smoothly through the ups and downs of social gatherings and during the ascent and descent of elevators. If an all time "top ten" of American romantic ballads were selected, "Always" would almost surely be toward the top of the list.

"Always" was also one of Berlin's five favorites from among his hundreds of compositions. The others were "Easter Parade" (the greatest Easter pop song), "White Christmas" (perhaps the greatest Christmas pop song), "Show Business" or "There's No Business Like Show Business" (the unofficial anthem of the American theater), and "God Bless America" (regarded by many as the unofficial U.S. national anthem). With such distinguished company joining "Always" in this superb quintet, it may not be inappropriate to dub "Always" as perhaps the finest love tribute in American popular culture. It surely will not be on the lips of lovers always, for even the best creations eventually disappear, but like its composer it will probably last far beyond the usual lifespan of popular music.

April Showers

You may possibly be reading this essay during a gentle April shower, but it was written in the midst of a diametrical weather event, a blustery, Midwestern blizzard. Understandably, few songs have touched upon the theme of a raging snowstorm, though many have displayed delight at the beauty and fun of already fallen snow. Probably the only famous song extolling the virtues of a wild winter storm in progress is the 1945 classic "Let It Snow, Let It Snow, Let It Snow" by Sammy Cahn and Jule Styne. But even in that charming piece, the reason for joy is the good fortune of being indoors with one's sweetheart.

In contrast, a number of songs have been inspired by April, including "April in Paris" (1932) by E. Y. Harburg and Vernon Duke, "April Love" (1957) by Paul Francis Webster and Sammy Fain, and, of course, "April Showers." A performance favorite of Al Jolson, "Showers" was created in 1921 with a breezy melody by Louis Silvers (1889-1954) and upbeat lyrics by Bud De Sylva (1895-1950). De Sylva also collaborated on two other Jolson standards, "California, Here I Come" (1924) and "If You Knew Susie" (1925), which similarly have positive tones and outlooks.

Few songs are as cheery as "April Showers." Mentions of "flowers," "May," and "bluebirds" collectively help you forget the temporary inconvenience of spring rains. In the same vein, might it be possible to compose a song to counteract the psychological effects of a midwinter blizzard? Well, judge for yourself. The words that rhyme with "blizzard" are "wizard," "gizzard," and "lizard."

Bill Bailey, Won't You Please Come Home?

On the way home, Bill Bailey, could you please identify yourself? Are you fictitious? Are you a real person whose exploits were chronicled in song? Or are you a real person wrongly accused of domestic difficulties?

There were several "Bill Bailey" pieces both before and after 1902 when the famous "Bill Bailey, Won't You Please Come Home?" was published. That suggests that Bailey was an imaginary person whose name was selected and perpetuated because of the "b" and "l" alliteration. But it is also possible that Bailey was real. One of the candidates for the honor is Williard "Bill" Bailey, a trombonist and music teacher in Jackson, Michigan around the turn of the century. Supposedly, the song was composed in Jackson. Another Bill Bailey was a vaudevillian in the team of Bailey and Cowan, and was an acquaintance of Hughie Cannon (1877-1912), the composer of the song.

With the circuslike style of this ragtime classic and the carnival of confusion about the inspiration for the composition, the origins of Bill Bailey could even have been derived from the renowned Barnum and Bailey Circus, which was formed in 1871. This suggestion was written mostly in jest, but it is not entirely absurd that the "B___ and Bailey" may have evolved into "Bill Bailey." In any case, for almost a century the Bill Bailey song has brought as much delight to persons around the world as the best of circus music.

By the Beautiful Sea

If you attended movies very much in the 1940s and 1950s, you probably remember "the bouncing ball." In a nauseatingly large number of animated cartoons, the ball bounced from note to note to guide the audience in a collective sing-along. Some moviegoers apparently enjoyed this form of audience participation, but to at least some others it seemed as if the bouncing ball sequence at the end of the cartoon was a way to avoid devising more plot and drawing more funny pictures.

One of the familiar songs utilized in these cartoons was "By the Beautiful Sea." With words by Harold Atteridge (1886-1938) and music by Harry Carroll (1892-1962), who was born by the beautiful sea in Atlantic City, New Jersey, the 1914 composition is one of the more successful novelty pieces in American popular culture. In addition to its interpolation in the medium of movie cartoons, it was also inserted in a 1914 revue, *The Passing Show,* and in several movies, including the 1959 classic comedy *Some Like It Hot.*

Because some also like it sensitive and romantic, Carroll also contributed to another well-known song. In 1918, he adapted a melody from Frederic Chopin and with new words by Joseph McCarthy created the ever popular "I'm Always Chasing Rainbows." As far as this author knows, that ethereal excerpt from the classics was never reduced to being embarrassed by the infamous bouncing ball.

By the Light of the Silvery Moon

Outside of love, perhaps no other subject has been romanticized in popular song more than the moon. Humans have always been fascinated by things lunar and have connected beauty, love, and craziness to the familiar astronomical body. (Is it possible that there is a relation between the last two?)

A partial list of compositions beginning with "Moon" would include "Moonglow" (1934) by Will Hudson, Eddie DeLange, and Irving Mills, "Moonlight and Roses" (1925) by Ben Black and Neil Moret, "Moonlight Bay" (1912) by lyricist Edward Madden and composer Percy Wenrich, "Moonlight Serenade" (1939) by lyricist Mitchell Parish and composer Glenn Miller, "Moon Over Miami" (1935) by lyricist Edgar Leslie and composer Joseph A. Burke, and "Moon River" (1962) by lyricist Johnny Mercer and composer Henry Mancini. These full moon songs, in addition, had waxing effects on the careers of their authors. "Moonglow" was Hudson's top song, one of DeLange's top two along with "A String of Pearls" (1942), and one of Mills' top three along with "Sophisticated Lady" (1933) and "Mood Indigo" (1931). "Moonlight and Roses" was the most famous composition of Black and Moret.

"Moonlight Bay" was one of Madden's best along with "By the Light of the Silvery Moon" (1909), and one of Wenrich's most famous along with "Put on Your Old Gray Bonnet" (1909, with lyricist Stanley Murphy) and "When You Wore a Tulip," and "I Wore a Big Red Rose" (1924, with lyricist Jack Mahoney). Moonlight Serenade was one of Parish's most famous songs, and Miller's musical signature. "Moon Over Miami" and "For Me and My Gal" (1917, with co-lyricist E. Ray Goetz and composer George W. Meyer) were Leslie's main pieces. It was also a top song for Burke along with "Carolina Moon" (1928), "Tip Toe Through the Tulips" (1929), and "For You" (1930).

Songs with "moon" later in the title include "Full Moon and

Empty Arms" (1946) by Buddy Kaye and Ted Mossman, "When the Moon Comes Over the Mountain" (1931) by Kate Smith, Howard Johnson, and Harry Woods, "Allegheny Moon" (1956) by Al Hoffman and Dick Manning, "Carolina Moon" (1928) by lyricist Benny Davis and above-mentioned composer Burke, "How High the Moon" (1940) by lyricist Nancy Hamilton and composer Morgan Lewis, "Shine On, Harvest Moon" (1908) by Jack Norworth and Nora Bayes, and "By the Light of the Silvery Moon" (1909), by above-mentioned lyricist Madden (1878-1952) and composer Gus Edwards (1879-1945). This shining group of songs also reflected favorably on their creators. "Full Moon" was Kaye and Mossman's best and borrowed from Sergei Rachmaninoff's most famous work, the second piano concerto. "When the Moon" was Johnson's top song, and one of Wood's best along with "I'm Looking Over a Four Leaf Clover" (1927). It also became Smith's theme song.

"Allegheny Moon" and "Takes Two to Tango" (1952) were Hoffman and Manning's finest, along with Hoffman's "Heartaches" (1931, with lyricist John Klenner). "Carolina Moon" and "Baby Face" (1926) were Davis' most famous compositions, and Burke has been referred to above. "How High the Moon" was Hamilton and Lewis' best. Bayes' top song was "Shine On, Harvest Moon," but Norworth and composer Albert von Tilzer also scored with "Take Me Out to the Ball Game" (1908). "By the Light" and "In My Merry Oldsmobile" (1905, with lyricist Vincent P. Bryan) were Edward's big hits.

Collectively these musical moonbeams, and a number of others, are enough to provide good fun and pleasure for many a moon. Incidentally, this essay was written (honestly) during a period of the full moon, which may help to explain its nature.

California, Here I Come

As large as California is in population and geographical size, it has had relatively few famous songs written about it. The lovely 1962 ballad "I Left My Heart in San Francisco" and the 1924 rouser "California, Here I Come" are really about the only well-known tributes to the Golden State.

The latter piece was a repertory favorite of the popular entertainer Al Jolson (1886-1950), along with "Swanee" (1919), "Toot, Toot Tootsie" (1922), "Waiting for the Robert E. Lee" (1912), "When the Red, Red Robin Comes Bob, Bob, Bobbin' Along" (1926), "My Mammy" (1921), and "April Showers." One difference with "California," though, was that Jolson himself was involved with the song's creation. He wrote the lyrics in collaboration with Bud De Sylva (1895-1950), and the music was composed by Joseph Meyer (1894-1987). De Sylva and Meyer also collaborated on "If You Knew Susie" (1925), which was also a Jolson standard, and De Sylva wrote "April Showers" with Louis Silvers. Neither Jolson, De Sylva, nor Meyer had anything to do with the composition of "Tootsie" (words by Gus Kahn and Ernie Erdman, music by Dan Russo), "Robert E. Lee" (words by L. Wolfe Gilbert, music by Lewis F. Muir), "Robin" (words and music by Harry Woods), or "Mammy" (words by Joe Young and Sam M. Lewis, music by Walter Donaldson).

Three other songs, though, that Jolson did popularize and also contribute to were: "Avalon" (1920), words and music by Jolson and Vincent Rose, but with a melody that a court decided had been plagiarized from Giacomo Puccini's outstanding 1900 opera *Tosca*; "Anniversary Song" (1946), words by Jolson and music adopted by Saul Chaplin from a classical piece, Ion Ivanovici's 1880 waltz "Waves of the Danube;" and "Me and My Shadow" (1927), words by Billy Rose and music by Jolson and Dave Dreyer with no borrowing involved.

If you think that song writing and the entertainment business are easy to understand, just try to memorize the complexities of the last two paragraphs. I'd rather just enjoy myself by belting out, Jolson style, the pleasurable lines of "California, Here I Come."

Casey Jones

As the railroad spread its steel pathways across the United States during the past century and a half, various songs have gone along for the ride. "I've Been Working on the Railroad," an anonymous 1894 American ballad, is probably the best known railroad concoction. However, "She'll Be Comin' 'Round the Mountain," a folk piece from the late nineteenth century that was widely propagated by railroad crews, is also a very popular quasi-railroad composition. A much later rail tribute, "Wabash Cannonball" (1940) by A. P. Carter, has steamed along quite strongly too.

The shiniest locomotive in the musical rail yards, though, may be "Casey Jones." Written in 1909 by lyricist T. Lawrence Seibert and composer Eddie Newton, *Casey* is not just a well-crafted engine to transport us to our destination of musical enjoyment. It is also a splendid recognition of personal heroism.

His hometown of Cayce, Tennessee provided the nickname for John Luther Jones. While at the controls of the Cannonball Express from Chicago to New Orleans on April 29, 1900, Jones died in a crash with a stalled freight train in Mississippi. In the process, Jones managed to save the lives of the rest of the crew by telling them to jump off. The incident reportedly inspired a ballad by Jones' black coworker Wallace Saunders, which was sung by black railroad workers. The white vaudevillians Siebert and Newton then either adapted Saunders' song or created their own version. In either case, the result was a perpetual testimonial to bravery as well as an enduring favorite of all who have labored or ridden on the rails.

Chicago

Great cities should have at least one excellent song written about them. New York has several fine compositions inspired by that huge, tough, concrete metropolis, and Paris, the city of light, love, and culture, has been honored many times. Similarly, the "city with the broad shoulders," Chicago, has twice been the subject of top-rate songs. In 1964, "My Kind of Town (Chicago Is)," by Sammy Cahn and James Van Heusen, helped liven up the free-wheeling '60s. In 1922, "Chicago (That Toddling Town)" epitomized the wide open atmosphere of prohibition era Chicago and subsequently became the town's theme song.

Although he was not a Chicagoan, it was fitting that composer and lyricist Fred Fisher (1875-1942) be the author of the famous ballad. Like so many early residents of the windy city on the shores of beautiful Lake Michigan, Fisher was an immigrant, originally from Cologne, Germany. After coming to America, he became one of the most prominent songwriters of the first half of the century. Besides creating the broad strokes of "Chicago," he also collaborated on "Come, Josephine, in My Flying Machine" (1910) and "Peg o' My Heart" (1913) with lyricist Alfred Bryan, "They Go Wild, Simply Wild, Over Me" (1917) with lyricist Joseph McCarthy, and "Dardanella" (1919) with composers Felix Bernard and Johnny S. Black.

Several of these songs appeared in Fisher's 1949 film biography, *Oh, You Beautiful Doll.* That indeed was a strange title since Fisher had nothing to do with the ballad of the same name. "Oh, You Beautiful Doll" was written by two of Fisher's contemporaries, lyricist A. Seymour Brown and composer Nat D. Ayer, in 1911.

Cielito Lindo

"Cielito Lindo" is one of a trio of popular Mexican compositions which have been well known in the United States for decades. The other two, "La Cucaracha" (1916) and "Mexican Hat Dance" (1919), are extremely lively and energetic and make "Cielito" seem like a lullaby or music for a siesta in comparison.

But "Cielito," with its famous exclamatory line "Ay! Ay! Ay! Ay!," is far from dull. The 1919 ballad, attributed to Quirino Mendoza y Cortéz, has a spritely rhythm and a jolly spirit. Part of the problem is that we in the north tend to think that all Mexican and other Latin American music must be as hot as chili peppers or as potent as tequila. Like Mexican food, however, Mexican music has its gentler and subtler moments. For example, one of the finest waltzes created in North America, "Over the Waves" (1888), is a Mexican piece originally entitled "Sobre las Olas."

In a similar vein as "Over the Waves," "Cielito Lindo," which means "Beautiful Heaven," is a love song. If it had a raucous beat like the other two Mexican songs, it would hardly be conducive to romance. After a couple danced to something resembling "La Cucaracha" or "The Mexican Hat Dance" for a while, they might not have much energy left for lovemaking.

Come, Josephine, in My Flying Machine

Some songs seem timeless. Others are very obviously dated. Included in this latter category is the 1910 novelty, "Come, Josephine, in My Flying Machine." Its creators, lyricist Alfred Bryan (1871-1948) and composer Fred Fisher (1872-1942), were, like the rest of the country, fascinated by the new technological gadget that had hovered over Kitty Hawk, North Carolina less than seven years earlier. (Later on, Bryan and Fisher turned their joint attention to "Peg o' My Heart" (1913), and Fisher by himself wrote "Chicago" (1922).)

Today, the term "flying machine" seems very antiquated and would never be used in a song except in satire or as a parody. But that is one reason why the ballad continues to keep flying. It is so quaint and semantically awkward that it remains a charming (and not totally unartistic) morsel of musical memorabilia. The only famous sound symbol of the pioneering days of aviation, it is a delightful curiosity from a time that seems centuries in the past.

What if Bryan had not chosen "flying machine" for his lyrics? What if he had written something like "Come Sweet Elaine (or Lorraine) in My Aeroplane," giving four beats to "aeroplane"? Would the song have been so successful? The melody is not the greatest, and the change to the less amusing term "aeroplane" might have dragged down the lyrics enough to prevent the song from really getting off the ground.

A later invitation of similar type was "Come Fly with Me" (1958) with words by Sammy Cahn and music by James Van Heusen. It is uncertain whether an airplane was actually involved in this ballad, but the word "come" was in common usage during the 1950s. For instance, there was "Come Dance with Me" (1958) by lyricist George Blake and composer Dick Leibert, which won a Grammy award, and "Come On-a My House" (1950). The latter song won no honors, but launched the significant singing career of

Rosemary Clooney and the lucrative composing career of Ross Bagdasarian, who later gained much attention for "The Chipmunk Song" (1958). Bagdasarian's collaborator on the 1950 piece was his cousin, William Saroyan, who on another occasion dabbled in drama and won the Pulitzer Prize.

La Cucaracha

"La Cucaracha," the bouncy animated Mexican novelty, is a song meant to be enjoyed. It is a delight to sing and a full festival of fun to dance. The extremely lively and invigorating tempo resembles the stamping of many feet to squash an invasion of repulsive cockroaches. Could it be possible that this was the original purpose of the enthusiastic little romp and stomp? After all, the English translation of the title is "The Cockroach."

A folksong of uncertain origins, it may date back to the late nineteenth century but did not apparently take its final form until early in the twentieth. First printed in 1916, it has been linked to the Mexican Revolution of 1910. If so, perhaps the cockroaches being eradicated were the overthrown leaders of the country.

Without any political or pest extermination overtones, "La Cucaracha" became popular north of the Rio Grande starting in 1934. Cavorting with new English lyrics by Stanley Adams, it was introduced in the motion picture *Viva Villa*. Soon Americans coast to coast were finding that "La Cucaracha" was an ideal method for counteracting the mental depression caused by the great economic depression of the 1930s.

Down by the Old Mill Stream

Down around the 1910s and 1920s, "down" was a frequent term in the titles of successful songs. The most famous was the old barbershop favorite "Down by the Old Mill Stream," which Tell Taylor (1876-1937) wrote in 1910.

But Taylor's downright lucrative composition was not the first in that era. Perhaps the most interesting "down" song before "Mill Stream" was a 1902 curiosity, "Down Where the Wurzburger Flows." On top of the comedic potential of the name and the strong possibility that the ballad has not been sung at all during the last half century or so, the piece by lyricist Vincent P. Bryan and composer Harry Von Tilzer has another fascinating sidelight. A successful follow up to "Wurzburger," by Von Tilzer and lyricist Andrew B. Sterling, was one quite familiar to beer drinkers, the 1903 waltz "Under the Anheuser Bush."

After "Mill Stream" came "Down Among the Sheltering Palms" (1915), words by James Brockman and music by Abe Olman, "How Ya Gonna Keep 'em Down on the Farm?" (1919), words by Sam M. Lewis and Joe Young and music by Walter Donaldson, and "Way Down Yonder in New Orleans" (1922), words by Henry Creamer and music by J. Turner Layton. The last composition should not be confused with "Down Yonder" by L. Wolfe Gilbert, another 1922 song. Subsequent to these pieces, "down" songs became less common, although hits like the English import "Cruising Down the River" (1945), words by Emily Beadell and music by Nell Tollerton, appeared from time to time.

During their era, "down" songs along with "gown" songs like the lovely waltz "In My Sweet Little Alice Blue Gown" (1919) by lyricist Joseph McCarthy and composer Harry Tierney, helped keep up the spirits of the American people.

Frankie and Johnny

Around the middle of the century, Frankie and Johnny were among the top male vocalists in America. Frank Sinatra crooned his way to the very top starting with his 1939 recording of "All or Nothing at All" and continuing for decades with rich baritone renditions of a variety of hits. Among these were "All of Me" and "When You're Smiling," both recorded in 1952, and "For the Good Times." ("All or Nothing" was written in 1939 by Jack Lawrence and Arthur Altman, "All of Me" in 1931 by lyricist Seymour Simons and composer Gerald Marks, "When You're Smiling" in 1928 by Mark Fisher, Joe Goodwin, and Larry Shay, and "For the Good Times" in 1970 by Kris Kristofferson.) Johnny Mathis came upon the scene in the late 1950s with a series of successful love ballads, all performed in a luxurious, smooth tenor, and similarly charmed music lovers for a number of years.

Frankie and Johnny were also around toward the beginning of the century. But in the earlier situation, Frankie had the higher voice because Frankie was a woman who had a tragic love affair with her beau Johnny. The apparently imaginary couple were immortalized in an anonymous ballad with a most confusing history.

Although some sources claim that "Frankie and Johnny" goes back as far as the mid-1800s, the earliest printing of the words and music together was in 1912. That version, even, varied considerably from the final well-known form, and the familiar line "Frankie and Johnny were lovers" did not appear until the 1920s. Many persons and songs have been linked in some way with "Frankie and Johnny," including the famous "Bill Bailey, Won't You Please Come Home?" It seems, in final analysis, that "Frankie and Johnny" is a gathering of bits and pieces that just happened to evolve into a classic.

Glow Worm

Lucille Ball was a very talented comedienne. Part of her comedy routines was to portray her character Lucy, on the long-running television program *I Love Lucy*, as a person with little musical talent. When Lucy tried to play "Glow Worm" on her saxophone, there was little glow and much impression of things wormy.

Usually when a song has fun poked at it, you can be certain that the piece has reached a significant cultural status. Such is the case for "Glow Worm," one of the more popular compositions of the twentieth century. Originally "Glühwürmchen Idyll," it was a number in the 1902 German operetta "Lysistrata." The melody was by Paul Lincke (1866-1946), a moderately well-known composer, and the lyrics were by Heinz Bolten-Bäckers (1871-1938), a motion picture and theatrical director. In 1952, the famous lyricist Johnny Mercer (1909-1976) devised some clever new English words and boosted by a Mills Brothers recording, the reinvigorated "Glow Worm" became a big hit.

As unique as the "Glow Worm" theme may be, there was another occasion when the production of light by beetles was the central topic of an American popular ballad. A few years after the German "Glow Worm" was performed in the U.S. (1907), a European composer who had immigrated to America was inspired to write a piece touching upon a similar subject. Rudolf Friml, born in Czechoslovakia, became a major figure in American music after the production of his 1912 operetta "The Firefly," which features the song with the curious sentiment, "Love Is Like a Firefly." (Glowworms and fireflies are closely related biologically.) Otto Harbach, born Otto Hauerbach in Salt Lake City, supplied the "Firefly" lyrics. The "Glow Worm" and the "Firefly" were the most famous beetles in music until the 1960s when a group of four Beatles from Liverpool, England dominated the world of rock music.

I'm Just a Vagabond Lover

Rudy Vallée was not born in a valley, but in a pond. According to the historical records, Island Pond, Vermont was his place of birth. His place of work, however, was the whole United States, for Vallée (1901-1986) became one of the most popular entertainers in the United States. With a college-boy image, and a megaphone as an aid, Vallée popularized several well-known songs during his career.

Among Vallée's standards were "The Whiffenpoof Song" (1909) with melody by Guy H. Scull and words by Meade Minnigerode and George S. Pomeroy; "As Time Goes By" (1931) by Herman Hupfield; "My Time Is Your Time "(1925) with melody by H. M. Tennant and words by R. S. Hooper; the anonymous "There Is a Tavern in the Town" (1883); and "Goodnight, Sweetheart" (1931) by Ray Noble, James Campbell, and Reginald Connelly. Another of his repertory favorites was "I'm Just a Vagabond Lover" (1929), which he composed himself along with Leon Zimmerman.

Except for "Goodnight, Sweetheart," this batch of songs is a bit strange. "Whiffenpoof" is an excellent piece, but with its lines about little black sheep going astray and about being doomed from here to eternity is decidedly esoteric and mystical. "As Time Goes By" is also a good composition, but not until it was used as a recurrent theme in the legendary 1942 film *Casablanca* did it become a hit. "My Time Is Your Time" is so corny and monotonous that it could turn stomachs. "Tavern in the Town," although quite well crafted, is a blatant drinking song. And it is hard to describe "Vagabond Lover" except that it is unusual. The inspiration for the title of Vallée's composition may have come from "The Song of the Vagabonds" (1925), which was a big hit just four years earlier. While Rudolf Friml's brilliant and vigorous "Song of the Vagabonds" may have been the king of the road, the other Rudy's lethargic and dull "Vagabond Lover" was much closer to being a bum.

I'm Looking Over a Four-Leaf Clover

When Mort Dixon and Harry Woods wrote "I'm Looking Over a Four-Leaf Clover" in 1927, it turned out to be especially lucky for them. A top hit of the late 1920s, "Four-Leaf Clover" was revived in 1948 again with great success. Since its debut, it has been a staple whenever Americans want to sing or hear more sentimental old-fashioned style music. It has even been parodied more than once.

"Four-Leaf Clover" was the four-star winner of Dixon and Woods' artistry and their only key collaboration. Dixon (1892-1956) away from Woods was the lyricist for three good compositions with composer Harry Warren, "I Found a Million-Dollar Baby" (1931), "Would You Like to Take a Walk?" (1930), and "You're My Everything" (1931). (Billy Rose was co-lyricist for the first two songs and Joe Young was co-lyricist for the third one.) Dixon also did the lyrics for two standard songs with composer Ray Henderson, "Bye, Bye, Blackbird" (1926) and "That Old Gang of Mine" (1923). (Rose again collaborated on the words for "Gang.")

Woods (1896-) without Dixon produced a few other hits too. "Side by Side" (1927) and "When the Red, Red Robin Comes Bob, Bob, Bobbin' Along" (1926) were entirely by Woods, "When the Moon Comes Over the Mountain" (1931), Kate Smith's theme song, was by Smith, Woods, and Howard Johnson, and "Try a Little Tenderness" (1932) was by Woods, Jimmy Campbell, and Reginald Connelly.

This essay has contained a potential delight for nature lovers. Woods, warrens, and walks, mountains and the moon, blackbirds and robins, roses and clover, all have been around to enhance your enjoyment.

Let Me Call You Sweetheart

Over the years, "heart" songs, relating to affairs of the heart, have pumped a lot of life into the stream of popular music. "Heartache"'s (1931), words by John Klenner and music by Al Hoffman, has been a favorite for decades. The same applies to "Goodnight, Sweetheart" (1931) by Ray Noble, James Campbell, and Reginald Connelly. "Heart and Soul" (1938), words by Frank Loesser and music by Hoagy Carmichael, is one of the all-time classics. "My Heart Belongs to Daddy" (1938) by Cole Porter, "My Heart Stood Still" (1927), words by Lorenz Hart (unintentional pun) and music by Richard Rodgers, "My Foolish Heart" (1949), words by Ned Washington and music by Victor Young, "My Heart Cries for You" (1950), words by Carl Sigman and music by Percy Faith (melody adapted from the French folk song "Chanson de Marie Antoinette"), and "Your Cheatin' Heart" (1952) by Hank Williams all have been impact pieces.

One of the most successful "heart" compositions was "Let Me Call You Sweetheart." Devised in 1910 by lyricist Beth Stater Whitson and composer Leo Friedman, "Let Me Call" was one of the blockbuster hits of its decade and among the best love ballads of all time. Its influence may partially be judged by the appearance of three other well-known "sweetheart" pieces soon after Whitson and Friedman's. "The Sweetheart of Sigma Chi," words by Bryon D. Stokes and music by F. Dudleigh Vernor, came out in 1912. "Sweethearts," words by Robert B. Smith and music by Victor Herbert, was a top number in the 1913 operetta of that name. And most of all, "Will You Remember," or "Sweetheart," with its famous line "Sweetheart, sweetheart, sweetheart" by Rida Johnson Young to accompany Romberg's gentle waltz, was a main factor in the success of the 1917 operetta *Maytime*.

"Let Me Call You Sweetheart" was not a one song phenomenon

either. Whitson and Friedman, prior to their 1910 giant, also came up with a sizable creation with the 1909 winner "Meet Me Tonight in Dreamland." It should be noted that this earlier composition dealt with an even more complex component of the human condition.

Mexican Hat Dance

It's probably not true that the "Mexican Hat Dance" was devised to copy the movements of Mexican jumping beans. But when human beings bounce around the big sombrero to the compelling beat, they are as active as the little moth larvae inside the Mexican seeds. Before there were expensive health clubs and videotaped exercise workouts, there was, for free, the "Mexican Hat Dance."

The most famous of various melodies called "Jarabe Tapatio," after the national dance of Mexico, "Hat Dance" was published anonymously in 1919. Quite possibly it was from the folk repertory. No Spanish words were published with the original, and no English words are known.

From the viewpoint of one who has several times participated in vigorous hat rituals, English lyrics should not be difficult to develop. With the experience of this author's earlier days in mind, the following lines are offered:

We move like in a trance
Around the great big hat.
It is a lovely dance,
There's no denying that.

But soon our tired feet
Will have to go too fast
To an up-tempo beat–
I hope that we will last!

My Melancholy Baby

Probably the most famous song with "melancholy" in the title, "My Melancholy Baby" or just plain "Melancholy Baby" has a history that could make anyone a bit sad. The song is usually attributed to Ernie Burnett (1884-1959) as author of the tune and George A. Norton (1880-1923) as author of the words.

But other claims and a lawsuit have complicated this otherwise uncomplex popular classic. Burnett and Norton published their composition in 1912. One year earlier, in 1911, Burnett's melody accompanied by lyrics by Maybelle E. Watson had been copyrighted but not published. Norton based his verses on Watson's "Melancholy," even using the same title until 1914 when the name "My Melancholy Baby" began to appear. Watson was Burnett's wife, but since they subsequently divorced and she won a legal battle over royalties in 1940, he could well be described as the melancholy baby of the song.

Another claimant was songwriter Ben Light who supposedly wrote the music in 1909 when still a teenager. In the often muddled world of popular music, where copying, imitation, and outright theft are common, Light's authorship is quite possible. But can you imagine the semantic deviltry that could be carried out if Light were the composer of this beautiful melancholy melody?

Oh, You Beautiful Doll

As the reader is well aware, Hollywood movie producers are capable of strange artistic decisions. In 1949 the biography of composer Fred Fisher came to the silver screen with the title *Oh, You Beautiful Doll*. The implication was, therefore, that Fisher wrote the very popular song of that name, but in no way did he contribute to the piece. If they wanted to use a Fisher love ballad for the title, they had readily available in the score "Peg o' My Heart," written in 1913 with lyricist Alfred Bryan.

Perhaps the title was chosen in part because the actual creators of "Oh, You Beautiful Doll" (1911) did not merit a movie biography. Lyricist A. Seymour Brown and composer Nat D. Ayer (1887-1952) wrote only the one standard, and one song artists are seldom immortalized.

Another one hit team were lyricists Edgar Leslie and E. Ray Goetz and composer George W. Meyer. In 1917 they cooperatively wrote the fine perennial "For Me and My Gal." (Meyer collaborated on various lesser-known pieces, and Leslie with others came up with some other enduring songs like "Moon Over Miami" (1935) with composer Joseph A. Burke and "America, I Love You" (1915) with composer Archie Gottler. If you were around in the days of old time radio, the latter patriotic composition was used as the theme for *Life with Luigi*.)

So how are "For Me and My Gal" and "Oh, You Beautiful Doll" related except for being love ballads from the 1910s? A 1942 movie musical with the title *For Me and My Gal* included five enduring songs. In addition to the title song there were "Ballin' the Jack" (1913), words by Jim Burris and music by Chris Smith, "Over There" (1917) by George M. Cohan, "How Ya Gonna Keep 'em Down on the Farm?" (1919), words by Sam M. Lewis and Joe Young and music by Walter Donaldson, and, you guessed it, "Oh, You Beautiful Doll."

On the Road to Mandalay

From the 1940s to the 1960s, Bob Hope and Bing Crosby were on the road a lot. Accompanied by Dorothy Lamour, the pair brought comedic chaos to various places and one non-place around the world via the medium of the movies. Their silver screen antics in *The Road to Singapore* (1940), *The Road to Zanzibar* (1941), *The Road to Morocco* (1942), *The Road to Utopia* (1945), *The Road to Rio* (1947), *The Road to Bali* (1952), and *The Road to Hong Kong* (1962) delighted millions. But one road they didn't travel was the famous road to Mandalay.

The second largest city in Burma was immortalized in verse by the renowned English author Rudyard Kipling (1865-1936), who was a native of adjacent India. Except for the 1890 poem by Kipling, most Westerners would not be acquainted with this exotic spot deep in the interior of the not very well known Southeast Asian nation. In 1907, soon after Hope and Crosby were born, the poem was set to music by Ohioan Oley Speaks (1874-1948), a singer and composer.

With its dramatic melody and esoteric oriental theme, "On the Road to Mandalay" has become a continuing standard in western culture. What other song can romantically carry us back to the place "where the flying fishes play"? It is never revealed to us what the strange fishes are playing, but it probably isn't the drums that are suggested in the rhythm of the music.

Say It with Music

That's exactly what Irving Berlin did all of his long life–"Say It with Music." He was not a great novelist or compelling orator. His medium of communication was the song, and he communicated most eloquently and often. Like William Shakespeare who with little education created a series of enduring masterpieces for the stage, Berlin (1888-1989) with little musical training created a series of popular masterpieces for the ear.

The introduction of "Say It with Music" was a good example of how Berlin's compositions had an impact on American culture. Berlin wrote the polished, free moving, elegant ballad for the first edition (1921) of the show, *Music Box Revue*. By then a cagey veteran, he decided to test the song at a New York night club before inserting it in the revue. His dry run almost backfired. "Say It" proved to be such a hit that Berlin had to squelch the performance of the song to prevent overexposure before the show premiered. Lots of songs have been "plugged" by publicists over the years, but this may be the only case when a song had to be "unplugged" by the composer to keep it from becoming too popular too fast.

You and I should have such a problem. You and I should have such a terrific talent.

She'll Be Comin' 'Round the Mountain

We all know that she'll be comin' 'round the mountain when she gets around to doing it. The famous song about her comin' 'round also took its own sweet time getting into print.

The tune for "She'll Be Comin' Round the Mountain," under the title "When the Chariot Comes," was published in 1899, and the lyrics, with the tune, were printed in 1927. But both elements were somewhat older. The music and the "Chariot" words reportedly come from an anonymous Black source, perhaps as early as the mid-nineteenth century. The "She'll Be Comin'" words possibly originated in the 1890s or even before, and were apparently a mountain folk adaptation of "When the Chariot Comes."

So this lively favorite, popular in the hills and in the flatlands, seems to be a blend of black spiritual and white hillbilly. Although technically from the second half of the nineteenth century, "She'll Be Comin'" in spirit belongs to the twentieth. Railroad workers, students at Southern Methodist University, participants in "sing alongs," and country musicians have all adopted this stereotypical symbol of mountain music.

Another well-known anonymous mountain song is "On Top of Old Smokey." Probably several decades newer than "She'll Be Comin'," "Old Smokey" was popularized by Pete Seeger in 1951. "Old Smokey" and "She'll Be Comin'," however, are about as different in style as compositions of similar origin can be. "She'll Be Comin'" moves with energy and a jubilant attitude, while "Old Smokey," in contrast, just stands around and complains.

St. Louis Blues

One of the finest compositions of the twentieth century is George Gershwin's 1924 classical-jazz masterpiece "Rhapsody in Blue." Among the themes from that work is a passage that is quite reminiscent of an earlier work, "St. Louis Blues." Since "St. Louis," which was written in 1914, was by 1924 a well known phenomenon, it is entirely possible that Gershwin's overall inspiration for his "Blue" was triggered by its "Blues" antecendent.

"St. Louis Blues" (or "Saint Louis Blues") is, like Gershwin's Blue, the most famous work of its composer. W. C. (William Christopher) Handy (1873-1958), a black composer who saw plenty of poverty days that made him blue, became internationally celebrated and financially well-off primarily because of this single composition. He wrote some other good blues pieces that were named after places (Beale Street, East St. Louis, Memphis) or persons (Aunt Hagar, Joe Turner, John Henry), but his renowned classic about the "St. Louis Woman" made Handy the dandy of his time.

"St. Louis" is one of the two Black jazz blockbusters of all time. The other one is the anonymous "When the Saints Go Marching In" (late nineteenth century). Both, curiously, have the word "Saint" in the title, although the earlier New Orleans piece never gets messed up by variant spellings of "St."/ "Saint." Could you imagine "When the Sts. Go Marching In"?

Swanee

Most of the top songs by George Gershwin (1898-1937) were complemented with lyrics by his brother Ira. The two exceptions to this were "Somebody Loves Me" (1924), words by Bud De Sylva and Ballard MacDonald, and Gershwin's first hit "Swanee" (1919). The famous words for the latter song were crafted by moderately known Irving Caesar (1895-). Although not nearly as accomplished a lyricist as Ira Gershwin, Caesar also collaborated on four other enduring songs. In 1936 he wrote "Is It True What They Say About Dixie?" with co-lyricist Sammy Lerner and composer Gerald Marks. In 1927 he wrote "Sometimes I'm Happy" with Vincent Youmans, and in 1924 he also teamed up with Youmans for "I Want to Be Happy" and the great classic "Tea for Two."

"Swanee" obviously owed something, at least the inspiration for the title, to Stephen Foster's celebrated "Swanee River," or "Old Folks at Home." It may even have been slightly influenced by Irving Berlin's 1911 classic "Alexander's Ragtime Band" which included an excerpt from "Swanee River." But "Swanee," a very distinctive composition, clearly had a personality of its own.

The same could be said for the great male entertainer, Al Jolson, who adopted "Swanee" as one of the leading numbers in his repertory, and for the great female entertainer, Judy Garland, who similarly embraced the song. Jolson and Garland were obviously not the only persons delighted with "Swanee," however, for none of his subsequent many fine compositions matched the financial success of Gershwin's first big burst toward immortality.

Sweet Adeline

One of the cutest novelty songs ever written was "The Alphabet Song" ("'A,' You're Adorable"), concocted by Buddy Kaye, Fred Wise, and Sidney Lippman in 1948. That little piece listed alphabetically all of the charms of the listener.

A similar musical listing, not quite A to Z, could be made for all the various females that have been mentioned in song titles. A allocates "Sweet Adeline" (1903), words by Richard Gerard Husch (under the pseudonym Richard H. Gerard) and music by Harry Armstrong, and "Once in Love with Amy" (1948) by Frank Loesser. B boasts "Bring Back My Bonnie to Me" (1882) by Charles E. Pratt, which remained popular for some time after 1900. C contributes "Charmaine" (1926), words by Lew Pollack and music by Erno Rapee, and "Candy" (1944), words by Mack David and music by Joan Whitney and Alex Kramer. D donates "Dinah" (1924), words by Sam M. Lewis and Joe Young and music by Harry Akst, "Diane" (1927), words by Lew Pollack and music by Erno Rapee, "Diana" (1957) by Paul Anka, and "Hello Dolly!" (1964) by Jerry Herman.

E elicits "My Darlin' Eileen" (1953), words by Betty Comden and Adolph Green and music by Leonard Bernstein. F finds "Fanny" (1954) by Harold Rome. G gives "Gigi" (1958), words by Alan Jay Lerner and music by Frederick Loewe, and "Sweet Georgia Brown" (1925) by Ben Bernie, Maceo Pinkard, and Kenneth Casey. I involves "Ida, Sweet as Apple Cider" (1903) by Eddie Leonard, and "Goodnight, Irene" (1936) by Huddie Ledbetter and John Lomax. J justifies "Come, Josephine, in My Flying Machine" (1910) words by Alfred Bryan and music by Fred Fisher. L loves "Laura" (1944), words by Johnny Mercer and music by David Raksin, "Hi Lili, Hi Lo" (1952), words by Helen Deutsch and music by Bronislau Kaper, "Linda" (1944) by Jack Lawrence and Ann Ronell, "Louise" (1929), words by Leo Robin and music by Richard A. Whiting, "Liza" (1929), words by Ira Gershwin and Gus Kahn and music by George Gershwin, and "Lulu's Back in Town" (1935), words by Al Dubin and music by Harry Warren.

M makes "Mimi" (1932), words by Lorenz Hart and music by Richard Rodgers, "Margie" (1920), words by Benny Davis and music by Con Conrad and J. Russel Robinson, "Marie" (1928) by Irving Berlin, "Maria" (1957) words by Stephen Sondheim and music by Leonard Bernstein, "Mary's a Grand Old Name" (1906) by George M. Cohan, and "Marianne" (1955), by Terry Gilkyson, Frank Miller, and Richard Dehr (from a Bahamian folk tune). N notes "Nancy with the Laughing Face" (1944), words by Phil Silvers, Johnny Burke, and Sammy Cahn and music by James Van Heusen. P points out "Patricia" (1958) by Perez Prado, and "Peg o' My Heart" (1913), words by Alfred Bryan and music by Fred Fisher. R recommends "Ramona" (1927), words by L. Wolfe Gilbert and music by Mabel Wayne, "Rose Marie" (1924), words by Oscar Hammerstein II and Otto Harbach and music by Rudolf Friml, "Rosalie" (1937) by Cole Porter, "Rose O'Day" (1941) by Al Lewis and Charles Tobias, "The Daughter of Rosie O'Grady" (1918), words by Monty C. Brice and music by Walter Donaldson, and "Second Hand Rose" (1921), words by Grant Clarke and music by James F. Hanley. S sends "Sweet Sue" (1928), words by Will J. Harris and music by Victor Young, "Sioux City Sue" (1945), words by Ray Freedman and music by Dick Thomas, and "My Gal Sal" (1905) by Paul Dresser. T tosses into the list "Tammy" (1957) by Jay Livingston and Ray Evans.

These and other compositions comprise a full bowl of delicious alphabet soup. In some ways, the first mentioned piece, "Sweet Adeline," is the tastiest morsel of them all. A long-time favorite of barbershop quartets and a continuing classic for almost a century, "Adeline" can easily be called the sentimental queen of American songs about women.

But enough now about the female gender in popular music. As lyricist Harry H. Williams and composer Egbert Van Alstyne wrote in 1911, "Goodnight, Ladies."

Sweet Georgia Brown

It's certainly not a great song, though catchy and plenty lively. Yet "Sweet Georgia Brown" has been heard and appreciated in just about every corner of the earth. Such extensive geographic proliferation is due to the decades of world travel and entertainment by the fabulous Harlem Globetrotters. The incongruous blend of basketball and comedy by this highly skilled assemblage of athletic clowns is, arguably, the greatest long-running sports show ever presented.

Almost lost in the barrage of hoops and humor are the original creators of "Georgia Brown." Little known Ben Bernie, Maceo Pinkard, and Kenneth Casey wrote the words and music in 1925. (Pinkard also wrote the tune of "Gimme a Little Kiss, Will Ya, Huh?" (1926) to go with the words by Roy Turk and Jack Smith.) As bouncy as the basketballs "Georgia" later was associated with, the little jazz piece has become one of the more familiar compositions in twentieth century popular culture.

When not being whistled during the Globetrotters' warmup exhibitions of ball-handling agility, it is being strummed on home ukuleles or belted out by dance bands. "Georgia Brown" has appeared in at least four movies, including the 1959 classic *Some Like It Hot*. If you like it hot and sweet, then "Georgia Brown" is for you.

Tiger Rag

Why would anyone want to hold a tiger? Sure, their fur is soft and their bold colorful stripes are very striking, but their claws and teeth are sharp and they have independent and unpredictable dispositions like their smaller cousins, the house cat. Calvin, the precocious and ferocious cartoon gremlin, sometimes holds his stuffed tiger Hobbes, but most of the time Hobbes is a fantasy conversationalist and mischief mate rather than something to cuddle.

The line "Hold That Tiger" in the chorus of the 1917 jazz composition "Tiger Rag" is certainly attention-getting by itself. But when the four Mills Brothers recorded the song in the early 1930s using their voices to imitate instruments, they quickly became tigers of the international entertainment community. Their rendition of the rag is decidedly one of the most unique and delightful sound treats ever impressed into wax. But even when not artfully manipulated by the Mills Brothers, "Tiger Rag" is a most lively and invigorating novelty.

The only unexciting aspect of "Tiger Rag" is its authorship. Like so many other good compositions, it suffers from the dullness of anonymity. An obscure person named D. J. La Rocca, plus the Original Dixieland Jazz Band, plus others have all been mentioned as the creators, but nothing is sure in the slightest. Trying to ascertain the authorship here is like trying to hold a tiger by the tail.

Wait Till the Sun Shines, Nellie

You may not have heard of the Von Tilzer brothers, born the Gumm brothers. They aren't the best known artists in U.S. popular music history, but, by gum, they did come up with a big mouthful of old standards. The older brother, Harry (1872-1946), wrote the music for "Wait Till the Sun Shines, Nellie" (1905) to go with words by Andrew B. Sterling, "A Bird in a Gilded Cage" (1900) to go with words by Arthur J. Lamb, and "I Want a Girl Just Like the Girl that Married Dear Old Dad" (1911) to go with words by William Dillon.

Younger brother Albert (1878-1956) was the composer for "I'll Be with You in Apple Blossom Time" (1920) with lyricist Neville Fleeson, "Put Your Arms Around Me, Honey" (1910) with lyricist Junie McCree, and the perennial favorite "Take Me Out to the Ball Game" (1908) with lyricist Jack Norworth.

The Von Tilzers did not invent the barber shop quartet, but they certainly helped to keep it going. Two of their collaborators, furthermore, also added classics to the barber shop repertory. Andrew Sterling wrote the words for "Meet Me in St. Louis, Louis" (1904) to accompany a tune by Kerry Mills. Jack Norworth was the lyricist and one of the composers for "Shine On, Harvest Moon" (1908), along with co-composer Nora Bayes. So the brothers with the pretentious pseudonyms, and their associates, were major contributors to the homespun, not so sophisticated barbershop phenomenon that entertained the nation before the days of radio and television.

What'll I Do?

The romance of Sam and Diane on the television comedy series *Cheers* was the main theme of the first several years of that program, which premiered in 1982. When the pair finally broke up for good after an extended tumultuous period of love, then hate, then love, Sam had a dream. He fantasized that Diane and he were an elderly married couple contentedly waltzing together. The music to which they slowly danced was Irving Berlin's wistful, questioning 1924 ballad, "What'll I Do?"

Berlin (1888-1989) and his big love, Ellin Mackay, had a relationship similar to the *Cheers* situation about 60 years earlier. Irving and Ellin's courtship did not run a consistently smooth course and during one of the bumpier moments Berlin was inspired to compose the beautiful musical inquiry. The song was added to the already-running 1923 version of *Music Box Revue* and soon became a refuge for lovers everywhere.

The main difference between Sam and Diane and Irving and Ellin is that the latter affair ended up in marriage (1926), no doubt aided by Berlin's considerable powers of musical persuasion. One of the pieces which probably helped convince Ellin was the extraordinary 1925 love pledge "Always," which was among Berlin's finest compositions. So Ellin was the focus of two of Berlin's classics, just as the annual *Music Box Revue* was the vehicle for disseminating two. In addition to "What'll I Do?" in the 1923 revue, Berlin's "Say It with Music" appeared in the 1921 revue.

When Irish Eyes Are Smiling

The Irish always manage to be a prominent part of various cultural activities, so how could this book ignore them? There have been a number of well-known songs on an Irish theme over the years, and the Irish tenor is a special breed of singer that is musical heaven or purgatory to the subjective ears of listeners.

Perhaps the most famous Irish ballad is "When Irish Eyes Are Smiling" (1912). The words by Chauncy Olcott (1858-1932) and George Graff, Jr. (1886-) and music by Ernest R. Ball (1879-1927) have been a particular favorite of Irish tenors. Prior to "Irish Eyes," Olcott by himself wrote "My Wild Irish Rose" (1899) and collaborated on "Mother Machree" (1910) with lyricist Rida Johnson Young and co-composer Ball.

Other "old sod" type pieces were George L. Giefer's "Who Threw the Overalls in Mrs. Murphy's Chowder?" (1899) which was a comedy favorite in vaudeville early in the century, James Royce Shannon's "Too-Ra-Loo-Ra-Loo-Rah" or "That's an Irish Lullaby" (1914), which was a favorite of Bing Crosby, "MacNamara's Band" (1917) by lyricist John J. Stamford and composer Shamus O'Connor, which was popularized by Dennis Day, "The Daughter of Rosie O'Grady" (1918) by lyricist Monty C. Brice and composer Walter Donaldson, which was a dance favorite in vaudeville, and "How Are Things in Glocca Morra?" (1947) by lyricist E. Y. Harburg and composer Burton Lane, which is one of the top pieces about the Emerald Isle.

Note that with the exception of O'Connor, none of the creators of these Irish standards are obviously Irish. (James Royce Shannon was the pseudonym of James Royce and therefore seems to be excluded from the Irish category.) Particularly interesting in this respect is the master of Irish ballads, Olcott, who as far as is known had no Irish background. Even his Irish-sounding first name "Chauncy" was changed from the decidedly non-Irish "Chancellor."

Whispering

As often as loving couples whisper to each other, it is surprising that there aren't more famous ballads relating to this topic than just one. But "Whispering" (1920) is the lone top pop that represents the secretive conversations of romance. Written by Malvin Schonberger (words) and John Schonberger (music), "Whispering" is one of the finer love compositions of the century.

"Whispering" became one of the standards of the Paul Whiteman orchestra, along with "Linger Awhile" (1923) and "Three O'Clock in the Morning" (1921). "Linger," a top selling romance ballad by lyricist Harry Owens and composer Vincent Rose, and "Three O'Clock," a good waltz by lyricist Dorothy Terris and composer Julian Robledo, were suitable repertory complements to the gentle chords of the Schonberger classic.

Two other compositions with a style reminiscent of "Whispering" are "Tenderly" (1946), by lyricist Jack Lawrence and composer Walter Gross, and "Twilight Time" (1944), by Buck Ram, Artie Dunn, Al Nevins, and Morty Nevins. All three are soft, smooth, intimate, and nocturnal. "Tenderly" refers to "the evening breeze," "Twilight" focuses on that transitional period of early evening, and "Whispering" by implication takes place during a quiet amorous evening.

Who's Sorry Now?

Since there have been countless love ballads written over the years, tears and sorrow are bound to intrude into them with some regularity. Wails and regrets have been popularized in such songs as "Cry" (1951) by Churchill Kohlman, "Crying" (1961) by Roy Orbison and Joe Melson, "Crying in the Chapel" (1953) by Artie Glenn, "Cry Me a River" (1953) by Arthur Hamilton, "My Heart Cries for You" (1950), words by Carl Sigman and music by Percy Faith, "I'm Sorry" (1960) by Ronnie Self and Dub Albritton, and "Who's Sorry Now?" (1923), words by Bert Kalmar and Harry Ruby and music by Ted Snyder.

Note that all of these pieces except the last one were created during the 1950s and early 1960s, a period of relative stability in U.S. history. Perhaps these negative-toned compositions were a counterbalance to the mostly positive trends of the times in the same way happy songs are rampant during periods of crisis such as depressions. Even "Who's Sorry Now?", the 1920s wailer, was popularly revived in 1957 by then unknown Connie Francis.

Kalmar, Ruby, and Snyder weren't always sorry in song. Kalmar (1884-1947) and Ruby (1895-) also wrote the non-plaintive hits "I Wanna Be Loved by You" (1928), words by Kalmar, music by Ruby and Herbert Stothart, and "Three Little Words" (1930), words by Kalmar, music by Ruby. Snyder (1881-1965) did not create any other especially notable songs. But he did have the rare experiences of writing tunes for some of Irving Berlin's early lyrics and significantly helped in Berlin's eventual climb to the ultimate peak of popular music.

POPS
1926-1952

Autumn Leaves

Autumn is the favorite season for many persons. The cool, crisp weather, football games, the World Series, Halloween, Thanksgiving, and probably most of all the incomparable beauty of fall colors, combine to provide a very special time of year.

Perhaps the best-known popular songs about autumn are "Autumn in New York" (1934) by Vernon Duke, "September Song" (1938) with words by Maxwell Anderson and music by Kurt Weill, and "Autumn Leaves" (1950). The last song originated in France, under the title "Les Feuilles Mortes" (translation: "The dead leaves"). The melody was written by Joseph Kosma (1905-1969), and the French lyrics were by Jacques Prévert (1900-1977). In 1955, the highly successful American lyricist Johnny Mercer (1909-1976) converted the French dead leaves into English "Autumn Leaves."

It is as an instrumental piece, however, that "Autumn Leaves" has become one of the biggest favorites in recent U.S. cultural history. When expansively performed at the piano keyboard with a dreamlike simulation of leaves slowly descending to the ground "Autumn Leaves" reaches its peak of excitement and color. Just as it would be very tough to duplicate the sensual experiences of nature's annual fall show, it will not be easy to match Kosma's elevating composition about things going down.

Beer Barrel Polka

In our modern public relations and media society, there are awards and honors for just about everything. If there were some kind of prize for the jolliest song of the twentieth century, "Beer Barrel Polka" would be a finalist if not the winner. Whether the exuberance of the song is due primarily to the uninhibited bounce of the melody or the expectation of a full barrel of brew about to make an entrance, singing or hearing the strains of "Roll out the barrel" is an occasion of extreme sensual joy.

"Beer Barrel" was one of about 70 songs, mostly polkas, written by the Czech composer Jaromir Vejvoda (1902-1988). It was created in 1928 when Vejvoda, in the unabashed vigor of youth, was the director of a brass band. Originally entitled Skoda Lásky (or "Lost Love" or "Pity of Love"), the song, with lyrics by Vasek Zeman (1909-), was published in 1934 and soon became quite popular in various European countries and North America. In German-speaking nations it became known as "Rosamunde." The familiar English lyrics were written in 1939 by American Lew Brown (1893-1958), who also collaborated on the words for the World War II classic "Don't Sit Under the Apple Tree" in the same very productive year.

There are two big ironies associated with this perennial favorite of the dance floor. First, that a song bubbling with so much happiness would have an original title suggesting sadness is indeed strange. Second, Vejvoda the polka master did not really know how to dance and never especially liked the dancing recreation that his music clearly encouraged. It is not known, however, what his views on beer were.

Blue Skies

The following is a test for history buffs. Taking into account the blue sky nature of Irving Berlin's ethereal favorite, "Blue Skies," and the composer's songwriting career from the 1910s to the 1960s, in which decade does the upbeat ballad seem most appropriate? Of course like most tests there is a trick involved with this question.

Berlin (1888-1989) wrote cheery music in every decade, no matter how bad the events of the day may have been. Like many other good composers, his music was not suffocated by the contemporary mood. The trick here is that "Blue Skies" was not written in an era of despair as the suspicious may guess, but instead in the roaring twenties, the most obvious and suitable decade of Berlin's lengthy rule as king of American popular music. The 1910s were marred by World War I, the 1930s by the Great Depression, the 1940s by World War II, the 1950s by the Korean War and the Cold War, and the 1960s by Vietnam and domestic unrest.

The carefree, bubbly '20s and "Blue Skies" match up so very well. Introduced in the already-running 1926 Richard Rodgers musical *Betsy*, the 1927 song sounds like a by-product of Berlin's imbibing of some bootleg prohibition bubbly. Whether it was that or Berlin's chronic romanticism, "Blue Skies" provided a readily available psychological boost for subsequent less optimistic decades.

Blue Tango

The tango, as suggested by Al Hoffman and Dick Manning's 1952 song "Takes Two to Tango," is a dance for a romancing couple. Therefore, the title "Blue Tango" is somewhat of a contradiction. But then, much about composer Leroy Anderson (1908-1975) was out of the ordinary or unusual. He was either a classical composer who won considerable fame in the popular music arena or a popular music composer whose works had a strong classical flavor. To avoid having to categorize him as either popular or classical, he is often described as a semi-classical composer. His music has been a staple of the Boston Pops Orchestra, which, like Anderson, more or less falls in between the two categories.

His compositions, in addition, are highly inventive pieces with frequently imaginative titles. The above-mentioned "Blue Tango" (1952), an instrumental with added lyrics by Mitchell Parish (1900-), is one of his best. There is also the marvelous 1948 Christmastime classic "Sleigh Ride" to which Parish also added lyrics after the fact. Plus there are "Bugler's Holiday" (1954), "Fiddle Faddle"(1948), "Serenata" (1949), "Syncopated Clock" (1950), and "The Typewriter" (1953). Among the various sounds focused upon by Anderson were a sleigh, bugles, violins, a clock, and a typewriter.

As a result, Anderson was consistently rewarded by the sound of the cash register. Nowadays, of course, the new computer registers don't make nearly as much noise, but the popular music of recent years more than compensates for that.

Boogie Woogie

"Boogie" is probably derived from the expression "boogeyman," meaning a scary evil character that carries off misbehaving children. "Boogie Woogie," in contrast, is a delightful musical experience.

An instrumental form of the blues, the boogie-woogie style of jazz was first recorded in Chicago in 1928 and quite possibly originated there. The famous composition "Boogie Woogie" was written in 1928 by a pianist with the exotic name Pine Top Smith. (Perhaps the label "Pine Top" came about from his sitting so long on pine piano benches.)

Although the names of both the song and its creator are more than a little unconventional, "Boogie Woogie" should not be sneered at. It is an innovative, skillfully assembled piece that has some touches of classical music. If it had been written by the renowned black ragtime composer Scott Joplin or the great jazz-oriented serious composer George Gershwin, "Boogie Woogie" might have gained a lot more respect.

Dance with a Dolly

There is a considerable difference between a huge, shaggy, basically unattractive buffalo (or more accurately, bison) of the American plains and a slender, lovely dolly (or more accurately, young woman) of the American nightclub scene. Yet the buffalo and the pretty dolly have both been immortalized by the same melody, "Lubly Fan."

Written by Cool White in 1844, "Lubly Fan" or "Buffalo Gals" became one of the most popular minstrel numbers of the nineteenth century. In 1940, the buffalo was transformed, like Liza Doolittle in "My Fair Lady," into a more polished contemporary dolly. The melody was adapted, creating a bouncy, lively swing piece, and words by Terry Shand, Jimmy Eaton, and Mickey Leader were attached. Among the groups that recorded "Dance with a Dolly" were the Mills Brothers, who also were musically acquainted with another dolly, "Paper Doll," their famous best-selling 1943 disk.

But in accordance with the old saying, "You can take the boy out of the country, but you can't take the country out of the boy," the twentieth-century dolly did not completely lose all the vestiges of her shaggy nineteenth-century predecessors. As urbane and sophisticated as the 1940 dolly was, she still managed to have "a hole in her stockin'," perhaps from all the dancing.

Deep in the Heart of Texas

Audiences usually clap their hands after performances. In the case of "Deep in the Heart of Texas," however, the audience claps crisply and briskly four times at several predetermined spots during the performance. It's a clever and lively song, which ensures positive listener response by the participation gimmick. In addition, the rapid manual activity and loud sounds are double insurance that the customer will not fall asleep.

You may ask why the people are clapping so enthusiastically. It's probably not because the 1941 novelty is a terrific piece. "Deep in the Heart" is fun, imaginative, and well-executed, but it is by no definition of excellence an artistic classic. You can also rule out applause for the achievements of its composers. Neither June Hersey, who devised the words, nor Don Swander, who wrote the tune, are really known for anything else.

Texans might claim that all the acclamation is for their proud state. This is feasible, though debatable. The truth is possibly that the audience is applauding themselves. After all, how often does one participate so vigorously and emphatically in the midst of a song? How often does one have so much enjoyment from one little old bit of music?

Deep Purple

It is clear what the "deep" in "Deep Purple" stands for. The deep, rich tones of this exceptional composition make it one of the very best American popular songs ever. But where does the "purple" come from? It appears, because of the sad "blues" mood of the piece, that purple is a darker, more intense variant of blue.

"Deep Purple" is the classic of composer Peter DeRose (1900-1953). It was composed as a piano work in 1934, was arranged for orchestra in 1935, and gathered lyrics by Mitchell Parish (1900-) in 1939. Two other standards by DeRose were "Have You Ever Been Lonely?" (1933) written with lyricist George Brown, and "A Marshmallow World" (1949) with lyricist Carl Sigman.

No other melody by DeRose approaches the fine, almost classical, quality of "Deep Purple." It was one of those little quirks of artistic history that an otherwise mediocre composer came up with a masterwork. Speaking of superlatives, the master of the baseball bat, Babe Ruth, loved this composition so much that he celebrated his last several birthdays by having DeRose sing it to him. Ruth, of course, gained his fame by hitting baseballs very deep.

Don't Get Around Much Anymore

The signature music of the great Duke Ellington (1899–1974) was "Take the 'A' Train" (1941). It is a bit ironic that Ellington chose this song as the trademark for his orchestra, for "'A' Train" was not composed by him but by his associate Billy Strayhorn.

Although "'A' Train" is an excellent composition, Ellington could have just as easily selected one of his own fine pieces. Among the possibilities were "Sophisticated Lady" (1933), words by Mitchell Parish and Irving Mills and music by Ellington, "Mood Indigo" (1931), a collaborative effort by Mills, Ellington, and Albany Bigard, "I'm Beginning to See the Light" (1945) by Ellington, Don George, Johnny Hodges, and Harry James, and "Don't Get Around Much Anymore" (1942), words by Bob Russell and music by Ellington. The melody for the latter was extracted from Ellington's "Never No Lament."

Much of the fame of "Don't Get Around" came from its burlesque-style treatment on the vaudeville and night club circuits. But there was nothing vulgar or ridiculous inherent in the song, which like the rest of the body of Ellington's compositions, and the man himself, was quite high class.

Heart and Soul

For whatever reason, young and amateur pianists love to pound the ivories to the pulsating rhythms of "Heart and Soul." Possibly it is because the song is not difficult to play, or possibly it is because this old favorite is one of the more compelling popular compositions of the twentieth century. With a music beat that resembles a rapid heart beat, "Heart and Soul" is catchy in style and sensuous in mood. The accelerated heart rate, of course, is a direct result of romantic passion.

The heart rhythms of the 1938 classic were created by one of the masters, composer Hoagy Carmichael (1899-1981). The soul was penned by wordsmith Frank Loesser (1910-1969), who frankly was not a lesser talent. In the same year the two super people also wrote "Two Sleepy People." At other times, Carmichael teamed up with various lyricists to produce "Georgia on My Mind" (1930) with Stuart Gorrell; "Lazy River" (1931) with Sidney Arodin; "The Nearness of You" (1940) with Ned Washington; "The Lamplighter's Serenade" (1942) with Paul Francis Webster; "In the Cool, Cool, Cool of the Evening" (1951) with Johnny Mercer; and "Stardust" (1929) with Mitchell Parish. The last composition is perhaps the best American popular song ever written and certainly is one of the most successful.

Loesser's other collaborations include "I Hear Music" (1940) with composer Burton Lane, "Jingle, Jangle, Jingle" (1942) with composer Joseph J. Lilley, and "In My Arms" (1943) with composer Ted Grouya, but it was as a solo act that he really showed his abilities. After being solely a lyricist for a while, Loesser took on the added role of composer for "Praise the Lord and Pass the Ammunition" (1942), "Baby, It's Cold Outside" (1948), and "On a Slow Boat to China" (1948), as well as for four successful musicals. This quartet of shows were *Where's Charley?* (1948) featuring "Once in Love with Amy," *The Most Happy Fella* (1956) featuring

"Standing on the Corner," *How to Succeed in Business Without Really Trying* (1961) featuring "I Believe in You," and most of all *Guys and Dolls* (1950) with several well-known numbers.

It is strange how the world of music works. Two top popular artists, more or less contemporaries, come together in one year to create a good standard, "Two Sleepy People," and a pop masterpiece, "Heart and Soul," and then go on their separate personal paths. Perhaps the more established Hoagy detected the latent composer in Frank and decided that one tune maker in a pair was enough. In any case, all turned out well for them and for generations of popular music afficionados.

In the Mood

The entire spectrum of human moods has been reproduced in songs over the years. Happy, sad, aggressive, withdrawn, romantic, lonely, serious, comical, and a variety of other emotional states are essential parts of the character of any composition.

There are three well-known pop musical works which specifically use the term "mood" in their titles. "Mood Indigo" (1931), by Irving Mills, Albany Bigard, and Duke Ellington, skillfully projects a downhearted feeling. The other two, in contrast, deal with anticipation in affairs of the heart.

"I'm in the Mood for Love" (1935), with words by Dorothy Fields and music by Jimmy McHugh, was one of several hits by them that clearly expressed what was on their minds. The others were "I Can't Give You Anything But Love, Baby" (1928), "Blue Again" (1930), "On the Sunny Side of the Street" (1930), "Singin' the Blues" (1931), "Don't Blame Me" (1933), and "I Feel a Song Comin' On" (1935) with George Oppenheimer as co-lyricist. (Note that in the rock era, there was another successful piece called "Singing the Blues," written by Melvin Endsley in 1956.)

The classic song with mood in the title, though, is "In the Mood." Like "I'm in the Mood for Love," it is a love song. But with its playful nature, as blatantly evidenced by the recordings that come to a soft apparent ending and then roar back in full sound one more time, it is also a fun song. Written in 1939 by lyricist Andy Razaf (1895-1973) and composer Joe Garland, "In the Mood" was the composition that brought the Glenn Miller orchestra its initial success.

Razaf's first big hit, ironically, expressed a completely different sentiment from the romance-seeking and mischievous "In the Mood." In 1929, he provided words for Thomas "Fats" Waller and Harry Brooks' classic "Ain't Misbehavin'."

The Last Time I Saw Paris

Like so many compositions about the capital of France, "The Last Time I Saw Paris" touches upon an affair of the heart. In a departure from the normal description of sexual pleasures, however, these verses reveal sentimental memories of a beautiful city falling under the occupation of the less-than-beautiful regime of the Nazis. Oscar Hammerstein II (1895-1960), who had a talent for lyrics quite worthy of the great metropolis of the arts, penned his tender tribute to his much-loved Paris in 1940.

His long-time associate, Jerome Kern (1885-1945), quickly supplied a haunting musical setting at the request of Hammerstein. In 1941 it was inserted in the movie *Lady, Be Good*, and as a consequence won an Academy Award. (Because the song wasn't expressly composed for the motion picutre, Kern himself protested that his piece wasn't entitled to the honor.) "Last Time" was also included in other films, most notably as the theme for the 1954 picture with the same title as the ballad.

Kern lived long enough to see Paris freed of Nazi rule in 1944, and along with Hammerstein surely was overjoyed when American, French, and other troops strode in victory along the broad boulevards. But he died only a year later, barely enough time to appreciate the liberation of the city and the great success of his fine song. In one of those strange games of fate, Hammerstein in similar fashion survived long enough to collaborate on another anti-Nazi creation, the 1959 stage masterpiece, *The Sound of Music*, only one year before his demise.

Love Letters in the Sand

The sands of time are sometimes represented by granules of sand falling down in a hourglass. Another similar depiction is a beach with relentless tides pushing sand to and from the ocean. Each symbolic representation reminds us of the unending flow of life from generation to generation.

Three generations are in some way involved with the ballad "Love Letters in the Sand." Nick and Charles Kenny wrote the words and J. Fred Coots wrote the music to this fine semi-philosophical piece in 1931. "Love Letters" and the 1932 Christmas classic, "Santa Claus Is Comin' to Town," created with lyricist Haven Gillespie, were the leading compositions by Coots (1897-).

A full generation later, in 1957, vocalist Pat Boone, a descendant of the famous Daniel, revived "Love Letters" in a top-selling recording. That was probably the highlight of Boone's singing career, which also included "April Love, Ain't That a Shame?", and "Friendly Persuasion." "April" (1957) was written by lyricist Paul Francis Webster and composer Sammy Fain. "Ain't That a Shame?" (1955) or "Ain't It a Shame?" was written by Antoine "Fats" Domino and Dave Bartholomew. "Friendly" (1965) was written by lyricist Webster and composer Dmitri Tiomkin.

On top of being a star vocalist, Boone also wrote the lyrics for the hit song "Exodus." After Ernest Gold composed an instrumental for the epic 1960 movie of that title, Boone the next year added words and made a Grammy-winning recording.

Pat Boone's successes made the career of his daughter Debbie Boone much easier. A generation after the peak of her father's fame, Debbie made her own hit recording with Joseph Brooks' "You Light Up My Life," one of the blockbusters of 1977. So, indirectly, Coots and the Kennys not only furthered their own causes with "Love Letters," but years down the road also gave boosts to the two Boones.

Mairzy Doats

In case you have never analyzed the lyrics of the gibberish novelty, "Mairzy Doats" (1943), the song is actually about horses, deer, sheep, and goats. If you convert the verbal games into straight-forward language, you get the lines "Mares eat oats, and does eat oats, and little lambs eat ivy, A kid will eat ivy too, wouldn't you?" Milton Drake got the idea from the slurred speech of his young daughter, and together with Al Hoffman and Jerry Livingston came up with this delightful hit.

Not all of Hoffman and Livingston's compositions were of this type. Hoffman also contributed to the love songs "Allegheny Moon" (1956), "Heartaches" (1931), and "Takes Two to Tango" (1952). Livingston (1909-), who should not be confused with his well-known contemporary Jay Livingston, wrote "A Dream Is a Wish Your Heart Makes" (1949) with Hoffman and Mack David, "The Twelfth of Never" (1956) with lyricist Paul Francis Webster, and "Wake the Town and Tell the People" (1954) with lyricist Sammy Gallop. The result of these three collaborations was one song of optimism and two of romance. Yet Hoffman and Livingston, accompanied by David, gave in to temptation once more in 1948 by producing another tongue-distorting creation, "Bibbidi, Bobbidi, Boo."

The composers of "Mairzy Doats" were not alone when it came to concocting nonsensical, odd, or unusual animal diversions. "Three Little Fishes" swam right over the dam in Saxie Dowell's 1939 hit. George Tibbles and Ramey Idriss' 1947 "Woody Woodpecker" mocked its way into the hearts of the public. The powerful "Mule Train" (1949), by Johnny Lange, Hy Hearth, and Fred Glickman, hauled a lot of loot to the bank. Terry Gilkyson's "The Cry of the Wild Goose" (1949) flew toward the top of the charts. And "How Much Is That Doggie in the Window?" (1953) would have wagged composer and lyricist Bob Merrill's tail if he had one.

Merrill also wrote people songs such as "People" (1964) with composer Jule Styne, "Love Makes the World Go 'Round" (1961) by himself, and "If I Knew You Were Comin' I'd 'Ave Baked a Cake" (1950) with Clem Watts and Al Hoffman. (There's that name again!)

Moonlight Serenade

In his lifetime, bandleader Glenn Miller (1904-1944) was one of the most appreciated figures of the swing era. His orchestra, with the unique, smooth "Glenn Miller sound" and a knack for having fun, charmed millions for about half a decade until Miller's untimely and still unexplained death in an airplane crash in Europe.

Among the top recordings by Miller's ensemble were the late nineteenth century favorites "Little Brown Jug" and "American Patrol," Miller's own "Moonlight Serenade" (1939) with lyrics by Mitchell Parish (1900-), "In the Mood" (1939) with words by Andy Razaf and music by Joe Garland, and "Sunrise Serenade" (1939) with words by Jack Lawrence and music by Frankie Carle. Other hits were "Tuxedo Junction" (1940) with words by Buddy Feyne and music by Erskine Hawkins, William Johnson, and Julian Dash, "Elmer's Tune" (1941) by Elmer Albrecht, Sammy Gallop, and Dick Jurgens, "Chattanooga Choo Choo" (1941) with words by Mack Gordon and music by Harry Warren, and "A String of Pearls" (1942) with words by Eddie DeLange and music by Jerry Gray.

After his death, Miller became a true legend of American popular music. The Glenn Miller orchestra, which was in the limelight for roughly five years under the leadership of the living Glenn Miller, performed big band numbers for five subsequent decades driven by the spirit of its founder. Miller was possibly the leading symbol of the big band period, rivaled only by Benny Goodman. His personal musical signature, the incomparable dreamy love ballad "Moonlight Serenade," is perhaps the most representative song of the time. It is certainly the sentimental favorite.

My Baby Just Cares for Me

"Baby," meaning a loving grownup, has been a theme in several well-known ballads with interesting chronologies. In 1926 came the initial sighting of "Baby Face," the bouncy favorite by lyricist Benny Davis and composer Harry Akst. Two years later, in 1928, came the suitor's excuse, "I Can't Give You Anything But Love, Baby" by lyricist Dorothy Fields and composer Jimmy McHugh. In 1948 "baby" finally got completely warmed up after Frank Loesser's "Baby, It's Cold Outside" appeared. Sometimes romance moves slowly.

Two other beautiful baby successes, in another probably unintended sequence, were written by the team of lyricist Gus Kahn (1886-1941) and composer Walter Donaldson (1893-1947). In 1925 the beginning of romance was affirmed in "Yes, Sir, That's My Baby" and by 1930 love was in full flow with "My Baby Just Cares for Me." But Kahn and Donaldson didn't just make baby talk. They also collaborated on four other standards, "My Buddy" (1922), "Carolina in the Morning" (1922), "Makin' Whoopee" (1928), and "Love Me or Leave Me" (1928).

When not working with Kahn, Donaldson wrote "My Mammy" (1921) and "How Ya Gonna Keep 'em Down on the Farm?" (1919) with lyricists Sam M. Lewis and Joe Young, "The Daughter of Rosie O'Grady" (1918) with lyricist Monty C. Brice, and "My Blue Heaven" (1927) with lyricist George Whiting.

Kahn also did well with others. With composer Egbert Van Alstyne he created "Memories" (1915), and with composers Van Alstyne and Tony Jackson he wrote "Pretty Baby" (1916). (Another "baby" song!) With composer Ted Fiorito he honored "Charley, My Boy" (1924), with co-lyricist Ernie Erdman and composer Dan Russo he concocted "Toot, Toot, Tootsie" (1922), and with composer Nacio Herb Brown he came up with "You Stepped Out of a Dream" (1940). With composer Isham Jones he wrote "It Had to

Be You" (1924) and "I'll See You in My Dreams" (1924). The last song was the title of Kahn's 1951 screen biography, which was filled with an abundance of Kahn's compositions plus a non-Kahn job "Ain't We Got Fun?" (1921), by Richard A. Whiting, one of Kahn's collaborators.

Oh, Bury Me Not on the Lone Prairie

The title of "Oh, Bury Me Not on the Lone Prairie" seems to be expressed in clear English. Yet the history of the ballad manages to alter or contradict every key word in the line.

The familiar words and music first appeared together in a 1932 collection of folk songs under the title "The Lone Prairie" or "The Dying Cowboy." A similar song titled "Bury Me Not on the Lone Prairie" had been published in 1907, but the music was different and the lyrics only partially the same. (Other possible precedents also were printed). The anonymous 1932 version, to confuse the issue, had probable origins in western North Carolina. Since there are no sweeping prairies in that state, the term "lone prairie" in the 1932 song is either mislocated by a few hundred miles or else is the product of a hill balladeer's geographically active imagination.

The 1932 version also substituted "out" for "not," thus creating a totally contrasting meaning. And in 1934 Carson Robinson created "Carry Me Back to the Lone Prairie," using quite similar music, and thereby supplying yet another semantic alternative to the "Lone Prairie" syndrome.

Whether you want to be carried back to the lone prairie, or be buried out there, or be buried any place else, and whether you prefer the imaginary prairie of North Carolina or the true prairie of the American West, you have an appealing song ready for you. If you are totally befuddled by all of this, on the other hand, maybe you would prefer big city music, which is never mind boggling to sort out. (Ha! Ha!)

Paper Doll

Paper is mass produced by paper mills, which can definitely not be classified as highly pleasant. The recording of the song "Paper Doll" was also a phenomenon of mass production, but by a far more pleasant experience–the fabulous Mills Brothers. For decades, Herbert, Harry, and Donald Mills, plus their brother John Jr. from 1925 to 1936 and their father John Sr. from 1936 to 1957, sang their way into the hearts of millions.

Starting in the early 1930s, they produced an almost unbelievable 2,246 recordings. "Tiger Rag" (their first record), the exquisitely rendered "You Always Hurt the One You Love" (1944) by Doris Fisher and Allan Roberts, "Lazy River," "Dance with a Dolly," "Glow Worm," and "Paper Doll" were their most famous disks. After Harry died in 1982 and Herbert died in 1989, the 60 years of musical charm by this early black vocal group realistically came to an end although the name of the Mills Brothers continued on.

"Paper Doll" was written by Johnny L. Black in 1930, but not published until 1942. In 1943, the Mills Brothers recording of it kept the record factories mass producing a million copies. The success of "Paper Doll" lay in part in the millstream smooth tones of the Brothers and in part to the unconventional nature of this romantic ballad. It's the only well-known song that extols the virtues of having "a paper dolly I can call my own" in preference to a fickle real woman.

Riders in the Sky

When researching material for this essay, this author at first got the impression that the well-remembered song "Ghost Riders in the Sky" was a spook phenomenon. Until persistent searching dug up the actual title "Riders in the Sky," the composition seemed as unreal as the musical portrait of specters on horseback stomping across the horizon.

But the 1949 ballad by Stan Jones (1914-1963) is as real and solid as its commercial success. The deep resonant voice of Vaughn Monroe propelled the dramatic and philosophical message of "Riders" over the million-recording mark.

Burl Ives, who was probably more at home with low-key folk ballads, originally introduced the song, and another top name, Gene Autry, sang it in the 1949 film of the same name. (A composition much more suitable for the casual country style of Autry, incidentally, was recorded by him in the same year. "Rudolph the Red-Nosed Reindeer," by Johnny Marks, became Autry's biggest hit ever. Note that both of these 1949 Autry efforts involved a group of animals moving through the sky.)

And what about composer Jones? Unfortunately, he is known for little else, and he was probably not "The Jones Boy" popularized a few years later in the 1953 charmer by Mann Curtis and Vic Mizzy.

La Seine

"La Seine" is a love song, but not the typical ballad about the attraction between a man and woman. It is instead the musical portrayal of the River Seine slowly meandering through the midst of its beloved and fully reciprocating city of Paris. The translated last line fully expresses the fundamental sentiments–"For the Seine is in love, and her lover is Paris."

One of the best of a number of fine twentieth-century popular French songs, "La Seine" was written in 1948, only a few years after the city had been freed of Nazi occupation. The smooth melody imitating the gentle flow of the waterway was composed by Guy La Farge, and the original French words were by La Farge and Flavien Monod. In 1953, Allan Roberts and Alan Holt devised a set of English lyrics titled "The River Seine" and yet another English derivative, "You Will Find Your Love in Paris," was created by Mack Gordon in 1958.

But the two American songs cannot completely communicate the thorough sense of affection that the French original conveys. On the other side, French translations of U.S. city songs such as "Manhattan" and "Chicago" would probably be similarly incapable of capturing the absolute personalities of the American communities. No matter, for we can appreciate the fine melodies in any linguistic environment and feel the universal atmosphere of love.

Stardust

There must have been some magical dust falling from the sky on that summer evening in 1927. When Hoagy Carmichael (1899-1981) was visiting his alma mater, Indiana University, the memories of a lost love quickly changed into the exquisite melody that has thrilled lovers ever since. A former schoolmate, Stuart Gorrell, who sensed the presence of stellar influences, dubbed the music "Stardust."

But Gorrell, who later wrote the words for the old favorite "Georgia on My Mind" (1930) in collaboration with Carmichael, apparently did not feel that "Stardust" needed any lyrics. Although he may well have been able to concoct suitable or even exceptional words for the new melody, Gorrell didn't take advantage of the splendid opportunity. In 1929, after the tune had started to become popular, Mitchell Parish (1900-), a lyricist on the staff of Carmichael's publisher, supplied a set of appropriate words on the suggestion of his boss.

Parish's after-the-fact wordsmithing continued with three other American pop classics–"Sophisticated Lady" (1933) with Duke Ellington, "Deep Purple" (1934, 1939) with Peter DeRose, and "Sleigh Ride" (1948, 1950) with Leroy Anderson. He also followed up the success of Domenico Modugno's Italian language "Nel Blu, Di Pinto Di Blu" with an English version, "Volare" (1958). But he wasn't always "Mitch-come lately." He also provided same-time lyrics for "Stars Fell on Alabama" (1934) with Frank Perkins, "Moonlight Serenade" (1939) with Glenn Miller, and "Dream, Dream, Dream" (1954) with Jimmy McHugh. It was quite a career for an unknown young man who just happened to be around when a great popular masterpiece came begging for lyrics.

Parish, however, wasn't the only lucky person involved with "Stardust." The song was Carmichael's first and biggest hit, and yet in its original form the melody did not draw much interest. It was jazzy and in medium tempo, and not until an arranger suggested a slower, sentimental style did "Stardust" turn into gold dust. Recorded hundreds of times, very frequently without lyrics (Gorrell appears again), "Stardust" is arguably the finest popular song ever to appear in American culture.

Stormy Weather

It may have been stormy outside, but the inside environment must have been clear and sunny. At a party in 1933, songwriters Harold Arlen and Ted Koehler "all but tossed off" their magnificently moody classic "Stormy Weather." Closely associated with the careers of Ethel Waters, who introduced it at the famous Cotton Club in Harlem, and Lena Horne, "Stormy" is one of the better musical expressions of the blues.

Arlen (1905-1986), one of the top popular composers of the twentieth century, and Koehler (1894-1973), whose most famous lyrics were in collaboration with Arlen, also tossed off several other joint standards. "Get Happy" (1930), with its jubilant line "Hallelujah, come on, get happy," and "I Love a Parade" (1930), the rousing march that continues to delight, were in a much more upbeat spirit. The 1931 ballad describing the paradox of being "Between the Devil and the Deep Blue Sea" was far from happy, but it had a lively rhythm. "I've Got the World on a String" (1932) was a clear projection of confidence, and "Let's Fall in Love" (1933) was certainly not an expression of negativism.

These five perennials, produced in a three year period, touched upon a variety of themes. "Stormy Weather," with its powerful hesitating tempo and deep emotions, is Arlen and Koehler's best collaborative piece. It's one of those songs that is so much a part of our popular culture that it seems like it has been around forever.

One final note that this pun-loving author couldn't resist. When "Stormy" was inserted in the 1946 movie musical *Swing Parade of 1946*, the female lead was, honestly, Gale Storm. Puns do occur in nature.

A String of Pearls

Strings come in many forms. There are the stringed instruments that dominate symphony orchestras but which normally are not used in dance bands. There are the strings of successes put together by outstanding big bands like Glenn Miller's ensemble in the late 1930s and early 1940s. And there is "A String of Pearls," one of the finer pieces popularized by Miller and his orchestra.

Written in 1942 by lyricist Eddie DeLange (1904-) and composer Jerry Gray, "Pearls" had the class of a succulent oyster dish and brought to its creators a lot of clams to take to the bank. But it was a rare pearl from DeLange and Gray. "Moonglow" (1934), a shimmering standard by DeLange, Will Hudson, and Irving Mills, is the only work by DeLange or Gray that compares with the perennial appeal of *Pearls*.

On top of making the world of pop music a bit more lustrous, "A String of Pearls" has made the game of romance a little more interesting. With the composition of the song, a gentleman has the option of presenting his lady with the lovely string of notes in place of the beautiful string of round white gems. She would probably be pleased by the music, but there is also the danger that she might decide to no longer be his woman. In the 1954 movie *The Glenn Miller Story* there is a scene in which Miller took no chances and offered up both types of pearl strings to his young wife. She was doubly delighted!

Tennessee Waltz

The typical country-western sound as exemplified in Nashville-style music, and the waltz, as perfected on the banks of the Danube in Vienna, are not frequently interwoven. In the "Tennessee Waltz," however, they blended together quite well. Written by Redd Stewart and Pee Wee King in 1948, "Tennessee Waltz" became a top hit in the early 1950s, mostly because of an immensely popular recording by Patti Page, and an official state song in 1965.

Another "state" waltz was the "Missouri Waltz." James Royce, using the pseudonym James Royce Shannon, wrote the words in 1916 for a 1914 piano instrumental by Frederick Knight Logan. (The tune may have been borrowed from an anonymous black composer, making Logan only the arranger.) "Missouri Waltz" was also a top hit and also became an official state song, but in addition had the distinction of being the unofficial theme of President Harry Truman's administration.

"Give-'em-hell" Harry was a two-song chief executive. During his campaign of 1948, the old rouser "I'm Just Wild About Harry" (1921) was used as a show of support. It's fascinating to see how Noble Sissle and Eubie Blake's 1920s comedy piece and Royce and Logan's 1910s sophisticated composition could join together in the 1940s as participants in the U.S. political process.

La Vie en Rose

During the nineteenth century, Paris was one of the premier sources for attractive and esthetic music. That fine tradition has continued well into the twentieth century. As if liberation from the Nazis in 1945 gave French people a new chance to be artistically creative, a batch of exceptional popular songs came out of France soon after the end of World War II.

In 1948 flowed "La Seine," or "The River Seine." (The music was by Guy La Farge and the English words were by Allan Roberts and Alan Holt.) "Les Feuilles Mortes," or "Autumn Leaves," fell into our lives in 1950. (The music was by Joseph Kosma and the English words were by Johnny Mercer.) That same year "C'est Si Bon" made us feel so good. (The music was by Henri Betti and the English words were by Jerry Seelan.) "Le Long de la Seine," or "Where Is Your Heart?" or "The Song from Moulin Rouge," warmed our hearts in 1953. (The music was by Georges Auric, and the English words were by William Engvick.) In the same year we strolled "Sous le ciel de Paris," or "Under Paris Skies." (The music was by Hubert Giraud and the English lyrics were by Kim Gannon.) And "Le Goulante de Pauvre Jean," or "The Poor People of Paris," enriched us in 1956. (The music was by Marguerite Monnot and the English words were by Jack Lawrence.)

Most important of all was "La Vie en Rose." Written in 1946, it was the first famous postwar ballad out of Paris and the most French in character. "Autumn Leaves" is better known in America, but is not generally known to be French. "La Vie," on the other hand, is the prototype recent French pop song and also a stereotype that has been commonly performed in a variety of movies, television programs, and so forth. "La Vie" is so very French that it retained its original title when Mack David (1912-) made an English version in 1950.

The composer of the rich, sentimental melody was Louiguy, the pseudonym of Spanish–born Luis Guglielmi (1916-). Louiguy also wrote the music for the 1951 song "Cherry Pink and Apple Blossom White," with English lyrics also by David. The sensitive French lyrics for "La Vie" were by Edith Peaf (1915-1963), a popular Parisian vocalist. Part of the reason for the retention of the French title in David's English rendering was the difficulty of translating "La Vie en Rose" into suitable English. "Life in Pink" or "Rose-Colored Life" doesn't quite capture the essence of the song. That is why alternative English titles have avoided trying to literally convert the words. Instead, such titles as "Take Me to Your Heart Again" have appeared and have to a certain extent managed to reproduce the intense romantic feeling of this classic.

POPS
1953 AND AFTER

Ballad of the Green Berets

The Vietnam War was probably the most divisive event for the U.S. in the twentieth century. An unpopular conflict fought half-heartedly for half-understood reasons halfway across the world in Southeast Asia, it divided Americans into antagonistic pro and con camps.

On the side favorable to the war was the song "Ballad of the Green Berets," written and recorded in 1966 by Sergeant Barry Sadler (1940-), an actual participant in the struggle. The piece was a big hit and became perhaps the most famous composition directly associated with Vietnam. It appeared toward the beginning of the war, when U.S. involvement was the most popular. As time went on, particularly after 1968, dissatisfaction with the war rapidly increased and various antiwar protest songs came more and more into public favor.

The United States' military action in Southeast Asia lasted from 1961 to 1973, longer than any other armed hostility in U.S. history. It was a period of unrest, cynicism, and disenchantment. The overall national negativism of the era is reflected in the almost total lack of significant new patriotic songs during that turbulent time. The sole exception, "Green Berets," was the last such piece to attract wide attention among the U.S. public.

It has been a generation since Sadler's ballad. Perhaps we are overdue for some more new musical tributes to our unique and great country.

The Banana Boat Song

Back in 1923 they had no bananas. At least that's what the musical curiosity "Yes, We Have No Bananas" claimed at that time. We suspect, though, that songwriters Frank Silver and Irving Cohn were not really commenting on the produce trade but instead were finding a new way to earn a lot of green bananas.

In 1956, in contrast, they had a whole boatload of monkey fruit. Erik Darling, Bob Carey, and Alan Arkin could have purchased the vessel and all of its cargo with the proceeds from their calypso smash hit "The Banana Boat Song," better known as "Day-O". Because of a 1957 recording, which made Harry Belafonte one of the top bananas in show business, "Day-O" further fed the calypso fad popularized by Belafonte with the 1953 Harry Thomas song "Matilda, Matilda."

In spite of the theme of a poor dock laborer burdened by the task of loading a ship, "Day-O" is basically an upbeat and good-spirited song. It contrasts strongly with the drama and pathos of an earlier composition, "Ol' Man River" (1927) by Jerome Kern and Oscar Hammerstein II, that also dealt with a similar work situation. The difference in mood was natural and very understandable. The man handling banana bunches had his freedom and some hope, while the man handling the cotton bales had neither.

Bridge Over Troubled Water

Over the years Simon has been going around saying various things. In 1967 Simon says, "We have a lot of heavy beat rock songs being written now, so I should compose an old-fashioned, soft, sentimental song as a cultural counterbalance." Well, songwriter Paul Simon (1941-) almost surely did not make any such statement, but a similar viewpoint was probably in the back of his mind when he collaborated with Arthur Garfunkel (1941-) on the lovely ballad "Scarborough Fair/Canticle." Inserted into the soundtrack of the outstanding 1967 movie *The Graduate*, "Scarborough" was one of the biggest hits of the late 1960s. With this song, plus Simon's Grammy award-winner "Mrs. Robinson" (1968), non-simple Simon and non-funky Garfunkel established their credentials as a top vocal duo.

Another bridge over the troubled waters of rock music back to the gentler music of bygone days was the very successful composition "Bridge Over Troubled Water." Written by Simon alone in 1970, "Bridge," an oasis of moderation and subtlety in a torrent of agitation and roughness, again bucked the trends and won a Grammy award. Simon was very deserving of this honor, because he perpetuated the creation of songs that not only appealed to the youngsters, but to parents and grammys as well.

Can't Help Falling in Love

In the world of motion pictures there was *The Magnificent Seven*. With outstanding action, good acting, tense drama, an exceptional score, and a morality theme, the 1960 western has became a cult favorite among some film fans.

There also was "a magnificent seven" in the world of rock music. That epithet is this author's description for seven successful songs that form the nucleus of Elvis Presley's famous series of popular recordings. There was "Don't Be Cruel" (1956) and "All Shook Up!" (1957), written by Elvis and Otis Blackwell, "Love Me Tender" (1956), by Elvis and Vera Matson, using a melody borrowed from a Civil War era song, "Blue Suede Shoes" (1956), by Carl Lee Perkins, "Hound Dog" (1956), by Jerry Leiber and Mike Stoller, "Jailhouse Rock," (1957), also by Leiber and Stoller, and best of all, "Can't Help Falling in Love" (1961), by Hugo Peretti, Luigi Creatore, and George Weiss. This beautiful love ballad, with a melody probably adapted from an old French love song, "Plaisir d' Amour" by Martini il Tedesco (1741-1816), was introduced by Presley in the film musical "Blue Hawaii." The movie, incidentally, should not be confused with the 1937 song of the same name by Leo Robin and Ralph Rainger.

Presley (1935-1977) was a controversial figure with a large amount of vocal talent coupled with a questionable lifestyle and dubious influence on the youth of his time. Even with the most negative view of "Elvis the pelvis," at least one redeeming factor shines through. Because of his sensitive, tender, and throaty rendition of "I can't help falling in love with you," Elvis can't be all bad.

Chances Are

The advent of the rock era in 1953 did not mean the total demise of old-fashioned, pleasant love ballads. Although the new style of music made such compositions somewhat more uncommon, sweet romance continued to survive in the new environment of increasingly hard beat and explicit lyrics.

One of the better pieces of tenderness in the early rock era was "Chances Are" (1957). With understated, gentle lines like "Chances are you think that I'm in love with you" and a quiet, meditative melody, the composition was a very appropriate companion for a couple in love. Lyricist Al Stillman (1906-1979) and composer Robert Allen (1927-) were not newcomers to the romantic music game when they wrote "Chances Are." They also collaborated on the affectionate ballads "Moments to Remember" (1955), "No, Not Much" (1956), and "It's Not for Me to Say" (1956), as well as the sentimental Christmas song "Home for the Holidays" (1954).

"Chances Are" (and "It's Not for Me to Say") were popularized by rising young singer Johnny Mathis. The velvet tenor tones of Mathis also recorded other good love songs of the period, including "The Twelfth of Never" (1956), "A Certain Smile" (1958), and "Wonderful, Wonderful" (1957). Smooth "Twelfth" was written by wordsmith Paul Francis Webster and composer Jerry Livingston who adapted the tune from a Kentucky folk song. Placid "Certain" was also written by Webster in collaboration with composer Sammy Fain. Exhilarating "Wonderful" (a personal favorite of this author at the time) was created by lyricist Ben Raleigh and musician Sherman Edwards.

These and many subsequent pieces indicate that the harsher atmosphere of rock did not squelch the production of soft or subtle ballads. Chances are such songs will be written until the twelfth of never, and that, as Lawrence Welk, the guru of old style television music, would say, would be "wonderful, wonderful."

Classical Gas

The Smothers Brothers spawned a lot of controversy during the turbulent late 1960s. Tom, the "stupid" sibling with the guitar, and Dick, the "straight line" sibling with the bass fiddle, have warmly sung and clowned their way into the hearts of millions of television viewers on various shows in 1965, 1966, 1970, 1975, and 1989. But it was their strongly satirical 1967-1969 program, during the peak of the Vietnam War and domestic political protests, that got them into trouble with the network. The show's contentious content resulted in its sudden cancellation by network executives, but Tom and Dick, who over the years have produced many laughs, personally had the last laugh because their social causes to a large extent eventually won the day.

The Smothers Brothers have also spawned the careers of many stars. From their infamous 1967-1969 "Smothers Brothers Comedy Hour" emerged future comedic celebrities Pat Paulsen and Steve Martin as well as pop music notables Glen Campbell, John Hartford, and Mason Williams. Campbell became one of the most successful recording artists of the late 1960s and the 1970s. Hartford's 1967 Grammy-winning ballad "Gentle on My Mind" became Campbell's first big hit and sort of his theme song. ("Gentle" quickly established itself as a top pop favorite.) Later on, songs like "Wichita Lineman" (1968), "Galveston" (1969), and "Rhinestone Cowboy" (1975) propelled Campbell into the top rank of popular singers. Jim Webb, who also composed "Up Up and Away" (1967) and "By the Time I Get to Phoenix" (1967), wrote "Wichita" and "Galveston." "Rhinestone Cowboy," a smash record in the mid-1970s, was created by Larry Weiss.

Perhaps the most artistic song having some kind of connection with the Brothers Smothers was "Classical Gas" (1968), by Mason Williams (1938-). A brilliantly lively and inventive combination of jazz and classical modes, "Classical Gas" has become, like the television series that gave Williams his big break, a minor classic of its era.

The Girl from Ipanema

Despite obvious national differences such as the dominance of the Portuguese language in Brazil, people in the United States tend to group the cultures of Spain and Latin America in one big Spanish lump. The music of these various countries does not escape this gross oversimplification, and therefore songs from these areas seem to blend together when they cross the Rio Grande. Often, the place of origin is uncertain or hard to discover.

Among the earlier good popular songs from Spain and Latin America were: "Granada" (1932) from Mexico, music and Spanish words by Augustin Lara and English words by Dorothy Dodd; "What a Diff'rence a Day Made" (1934), music by Maria Grever and English words by Stanley Adams from the Spanish lyrics "Cuando Vuelva a Tu Lado"; "Brazil" (1939) from Brazil, music by Ary Barroso and English words by Bob Russell from the Portuguese lyrics "Arquelo do Brasil"; "Frenesi" (1939), music and Spanish words by Alberto Dominguez and English words by Ray Charles and S. K. Russell; and "Perfidia" (1941), music and words by Dominguez and Milton Leeds. Incidentally, actor John Wayne reportedly had the emphatic "Granada" at the top of his list of least-liked compositions.

Among the later songs were: "Amor" (1944), music by Gabriel Ruiz with Spanish words by Ricardo Lopez Mendez and English words by Sunny Skylar; "Cuanto le Gusta" (1947), music by Ruiz and English words by Ray Gilbert; and "The Girl from Ipanema" (1963) from Brazil, music and English words by Antonio Carlos Jobim, Vinicius de Moraes, and Norman Gimbel. The last song, a big hit in 1964, is an interesting example of how a song can readily flow from one culture to another without the slightest pause. Incidentally, there also was "The Boy From Ipanema," a parody by Stephen Sondheim in the 1966 production "The Mad Show."

To complete this Hispanic tale of cultural confusion, three other songs should be mentioned. "Lady of Spain" (1931), words by Erell Reaves and music by Tolchard Evans, is a totally American waltz with a Spanish flavor. "Vaya Con Dios" (1953), a Spanish titled ballad, was written in the U.S. by Larry Russell, Inez James, and Buddy Pepper. And curiously, the fine 1925 tango "Jealousy" (originally "Jalousie"), often included in Latin American anthologies, was composed by Jacob Gade, a Dane.

Good Vibrations

Good vibrations are what millions have received from the multimillion-selling recordings of the Beach Boys. Originally consisting of the three Wilson brothers, Brian, Carl, and Dennis, along with cousin Mike Love and friend Al Jardine, the innovative style of the group has made the Beach Boys something truly special. With complex harmonies, use of high falsetto, and a breezy, casual demeanor coupled with a series of good songs, the Boys became almost supermen on the big beach of pop music.

Among their hits were "Surfin' USA" (1963) by Chuck Berry, and Brian Wilson's three mini-classics "I Get Around" (1964), "California Girls" (1965), and "Good Vibrations" (1966) (coauthored with cousin Mike). The last song is their best piece, as well as being one of the more brilliant popular songs ever devised. Unfortunately, at about the same moment that "Good Vibrations" was creating good times, the fortunes of the group began to decline. In part the downside was due to the emergence of a rival vocal foursome also beginning with the letters BEA. The lads from Liverpool, the rock phenomenon called The Beatles, became an even bigger attraction than the boys from the beach soon after the Wilsons and company had generated their giant wave of success.

In the long run, however, the Beach Boys had the last lyric. The big bug spray of life, triggered by ego and excessive success, dispersed the short-lived Beatles by 1970 while the clean-cut Americans surfed on as a viable ensemble throughout the 1970s and 1980s.

He's Got the Whole World in His Hands

Trying to categorize songs can be a tricky enterprise. Even when the origins and history of a piece are clearly understood, multiple places, time periods, and usages can make the composite cultural portrait of a composition subject to a wide variety of interpretations.

Even simple pieces like "He's Got the Whole World in His Hands" readily contribute to the boundless world of ongoing confusion. "Whole World" is a black spiritual, possibly from Alabama, probably of nineteenth-century origins, which was first published in 1927. So why is this pre-twentieth-century religious composition being discussed in a section on recent popular songs?

Until it was revived as a popular song in 1958, "Whole World" was a relatively obscure, minor concoction. Within a few years it would find a very comfortable home in the socially conscious, activist, civil rights movement of the 1960s. The lyrics were completely compatible with the cultural mood of the times, and the strong rhythm and lively attitude blended in well with the brash new style of rock and roll music. In some ways it is similar to the 1971 pop rock classic musical *Jesus Christ, Superstar*, which unconventionally represented religious themes in a 1960s context. "Whole World" was not a creation of that turbulent decade, but was largely a creature of the period.

I Left My Heart in San Francisco

San Francisco has been called, with much justification, the most attractive community in the United States. Yet two other major population centers were honored by famous ballads long before the pretty city by the bay. Chicago was given a musical tribute by the 1922 composition "Chicago," and New York City received multiple homages with "The Sidewalks of New York" (1894), "Manhattan" (1925), and "New York, New York" (1944). It wasn't until 1962, however, that Frisco was linked with a highly successful popular song.

The smooth, sentimental chords of "I Left My Heart in San Francisco," by Douglass A. Cross and George Cory, has become such a splendid standard that it is a little hard to believe it has only been around for about one generation. The melody had been published with different lyrics in 1954, but that combination had gone nowhere. After new lyrics were developed in 1962, struggling vocalist Tony Bennett, against advice, introduced "San Francisco" at the Fairmont Hotel in the city. In a very short time, after a three-million selling-recording, Bennett became an established star and the community finally had a song worthy of its natural and man-made beauty.

Unfortunately, San Francisco's late arrival to the realm of top popular music was also accompanied by a corresponding delay in its big natural disasters. The giant earthquake of 1906 and the serious tremor of 1989 occurred a lot later than New York's major fires of the 1770s and 1835 and Chicago's great conflagration of 1871. New York's and Chicago's tragedies took place while the towns were still relatively small, but Frisco's two deadly shake-ups arrived after the area had grown to a large metropolis. The song was worth waiting for. The seismic mischief was not.

I Want to Hold Your Hand

Insects do not live long, but they do have a substantial impact on humans. Likewise, the 1960s rock group, which partially derived their double entendre name from an order of insects, was not together for many years and yet left behind a very large pop music legacy.

Liverpool natives John Lennon, Paul McCartney, George Harrison, and Ringo Starr all were around 20 years old when they had their first successful recording in 1962. By 1963 The Beatles were a tremendous sensation and Beatlemania was becoming one of the big fads of the period. But after 1967 the group was starting to fall apart and by 1970 the brief existence of the species was no more. The death of John Lennon in 1980 completely sealed the faint possibility of a reconciliation. Solo careers after 1970, particularly that of Paul McCartney, did achieve some degree of success, but as separate entertainers the ex-Beatles did not begin to approach the dizzying altitude of the mid-1960s.

In their several years of frenetic joint activity, the Beatles engendered an ongoing cult following and several good songs. Their best composition is probably the 1964 love ballad "I Want to Hold Your Hand," which came at the height of the hysteria. With touches of classical music bolstering this enormous hit created by Lennon (1940-1980) and McCartney (1942-), the critical reaction was overall very positive. "Hold Your Hand" received the Ivor Novello Award and was even performed by the Boston Pops Orchestra. Lennon and McCartney's "Yesterday" (1965), "A Hard Day's Night" (1964), and "Yellow Submarine" (1966), all three of which also won the Novello Award, and "Sergeant Pepper's Lonely Hearts Club Band" (1967) were major contributors to the group's reputation too. Soon after, though, with their legend firmly established, the four young men who rapidly rose from the cesspools of Liverpool to the swimming pools of stardom, scurried on their separate ways.

I Write the Songs

Some years ago there was a story floating around about a man who was very curious as to the origins of the countless off-color, erotic, or dirty jokes that are endlessly circulated through our society. So the man decided to investigate the phenomenon by tracing backwards, person by person, the source of several such jokes. After years of effort he managed to discover, to his amazement, that all the x-rated humor was the creation of one unimpressive old man sitting at a desk in a small, dingy out-of-the-way room.

In a similar fashion, if you ever have wondered who writes all the thousands of popular songs we hear in our lifetimes, you might expect to get a clue from the smooth ballad "I Write the Songs." With a claim like that you would think that the composer was an endless fountain of pleasing music. But in another of the many strange quirks of existence, the author of the 1976 song, Bruce Johnston, did not create any other songs of note. Though the piece won a Grammy award and has been popularized by the well-known composer Barry Manilow, Johnston's successful contributions to American popular music seem to start and stop with his one song.

Perhaps a more appropriate title for the composition should be "I write the song" (singular).

It Was a Very Good Year

"Moments to Remember" was a successful 1955 song by lyricist Al Stillman and composer Robert Allen. Among the other moments to remember in American popular music were "Five Minutes More" (1946), which counted passion by the minute, "One Hour with You" (1932), which treasured romance by the hour, "What a Diff'rence a Day Made" (1934), which delighted in having a whole day, "It Was a Very Good Year" (1961), which stretched it out for 365 days, and "Always" (1925), which went on indefinitely.

"Minutes" was written by lyricist Sammy Cahn and composer Jule Styne, "Hour" was written by lyricist Leo Robin and composer Richard A. Whiting, "Day" was written by composer Maria Grever under the original title "Cuando Vuelva a Tu Lado" (with English lyrics added by Stanley Adams), "Year" was written by Ervin Drake, and "Always" by Irving Berlin.

Musically, "It Was a Very Good Year" really does not have a very good tune. But the nostalgic lyrics are very well-crafted and in combination with an adequate melody produce a quite pleasant vehicle for the enjoyment of reminiscences. Another such song of the same decade was "Those Were the Days" (1968). From an East European folk tune Gene Raskin developed this rousing tribute to times gone by. In style it was considerably different from the placid, low-key "Very Good Year."

Yet in intent they were traveling companions down the sweet, fuzzy road to the past where they joined other musical comrades such as "Memories Are Made of This" (1955), "The Way We Were" (1973), and "Memories" (1915). The 1955 piece by Terry Gilkyson, Richard Dehr, and Frank Miller was one of the better recollections of earlier experiences, and the 1973 Oscar and Grammy winner by lyricists Alan and Marilyn Bergman and composer Marvin Hamlisch was a fine misty backwards link. But the most gentle and kindly granddaddy of them all was lyricist Gus Kahn's and composer Egbert Van Alstyne's 1915 classic.

Love and Marriage

When Oscar Hammerstein II created the charming love novelty "The Surrey with the Fringe on Top" for the 1943 show *Oklahoma!*, he chose the term "surrey" rather than "carriage." Since the musical's scene involved a budding courtship rather than a long-term commitment, Hammerstein apparently saw the advantage of using "surrey" to rhyme with "scurry" and "hurry" rather than "carriage" whose sole suitable rhyme mate is "marriage."

Twelve years later, though, when Sammy Cahn (1913-1992) was writing a ballad about marriage, he not only utilized the obvious rhyming word but also created a pop classic. With the cute comparison of love and marriage going "together like a horse and carriage," Cahn's lyrics, hitched up to an appropriately rhythmic melody by James Van Heusen (1913-1990), became the Emmy Award-winning composition "Love and Marriage." Van Heusen's tune had a slower, heavier beat to correspond with the deliberate motions of a substantial carriage in comparison with the faster, lighter tempo used to simulate the smaller buggy in Richard Rodgers' tune for "Surrey." Van Heusen's music also matched the more reflective mood of its situation. Both words and melody of "Love and Marriage" were compatible with the conservative hometown atmosphere of the 1955 TV adaption of Thornton Wilder's *Our Town*, for which it was written. A later usage, however, as the opening theme for the controversial TV comedy series *Married with Children* (late 1980s-early 1990s), was definitely satirical since the family involved was far from the ideal of domestic bliss.

There are other synonyms for carriage, of course. But somehow cart, buggy, and wagon do not quite make it as semantics for romance. Can you image lines like "I lost my heart, In a pony cart," "I got my huggy, In a little buggy," or "Our love was draggin', In an old farm wagon"?

Love Me Tender

The reign of kings can be long and tranquil, or short and turbulent. For the king of rock and roll, Elvis Presley (1935-1977), his time on top brought an incredible amount of fame and wealth, but also a disturbed life and an early death. However, he left behind a number of good recordings that continue to be played as part of the ongoing Elvis cult, and some worthwhile songs that he actually wrote himself.

"Don't Be Cruel," one of The King's biggest successes, was written by Elvis and Otis Blackwell in 1956. A year later, the same two joined talents on the hit "All Shook Up!" (1957). Another collaborator was Vera Matson, who co-produced Elvis' best creation, the fine romantic ballad "Love Me Tender." The melody was directly borrowed from a much earlier song, "Aura Lea," which was written in 1861 by George R. Poulton (music) and William W. Fosdick (words). Whether as a Civil War era favorite describing "When the blackbird in the spring, On the willow tree" or a Cold War era hit requesting "Love me tender, love me sweet, Never let me go," the strains of "Aura Lea/Love Me Tender" are pleasant, sentimental, and soothing.

One of the Elvis legends that refuses to die is Elvis' refusal to die on the date alleged. If this is so and The King is still alive and in hiding, may the song he renders upon resurfacing be nothing less than his own gentle creation, "Love Me Tender."

Misty

In the somewhat bizarre 1971 movie *Play Misty for Me*, the definitely odd main female character would repeatedly request that the main male character, a radio disc jockey, air the 1955 love ballad "Misty." The dreamy song got a lot of publicity from the film, but associating the composition by musician Erroll Garner (1923-1977) and lyricist Johnny Burke (1908-1964) with a neurotic may not have been terribly complimentary.

Burke, not to be confused with composer Joseph A. Burke, who was more or less a contemporary, wrote several other well-known pieces. In 1936 he collaborated with composer Arthur Johnston on "Pennies from Heaven." With composer James Van Heusen he wrote "Imagination" (1940), a fine standard; "Going My Way" (1944), the title song of the sentimental Bing Crosby movie; "Swinging on a Star" (1944), the Academy Award winner that was introduced in the same film; and "But Beautiful" (1947), a good tidbit of romance.

"Misty" did not officially get an award, but it ranks as one of the best-crafted compositions of its type. If you are at all in a soft and receptive mood, "Misty" has a good chance of making your eyes and your brain misty. It's very easy to listen to and additionally has a fair amount of depth or introspection. No wonder the film producers chose "Misty" as the focus of the figuratively out-of-focus movie.

Never on Sunday

1960 was a busy year for a certain lively, very danceable song. It started out as a Greek language composition, "Ta Pedhia Tou Pirea" ("The Children of Piraeus"), with words and music by Manos Hadjidakis (1925-). Then it moved to France with new French words, "Les enfants du Paris" ("The Children of Paris"). Soon after it was on the other side of the Atlantic with a set of English words, "Never on Sunday." About the same time it was the instrumental theme of the successful Greek-made movie *Never on Sunday.*

The song that went from town to town in such rapid fashion had a man named Towne involved in its history. Bill Towne, an obscure lyricist, wrote the English words about the devout prostitute who would not think of selling her services on the Sabbath. The appeal of this seemingly contradictory philosophy, linked with a catchy tune with a true Greek flavor, made "Never on Sunday" one of the big hits of 1960 as well as one of the perennial standards ever since. Although relatively recent, it has long since attained the status of "golden oldie" and, heaven forbid, elevator music and its even worse cousin, telephone "on hold" music.

Olympic Fanfare

Since World War II, sports have developed into a very big business. Just about every variety of athletic competition, amateur and professional, is currently given a lot of audience and media attention. In tandem with the increased interest in the contests themselves, various sports specialties such as sports journalism and sports medicine have come into prominence.

One sports specialty that has yet to blossom fully is sports music. As time goes on, though, more and more pieces of music are specifically composed for or are commonly associated with particular sporting events. For example, Stephen Foster's "My Old Kentucky Home" is played at the annual running of the Kentucky Derby. The Harlem Globetrotters introduce their perennial basketball antics with "Sweet Georgia Brown." In 1985, players on the Chicago Bears performed the "Super Bowl Shuffle," which bragged in advance about their upcoming football championship. (The "Shuffle" was created by composers Bobby Daniels and L. Barry, and lyricists Richard E. Meyer and M. Owens.) And of course there are the numerous college fight songs that boisterously encourage the local teams on to victory.

One of the more famous sports music compositions is the low-key, sort of regal fanfare utilized by ABC-TV as the theme for their coverage of the Olympic Games since 1968. It has no official status with the Olympics, yet it has become very familiar to television viewers worldwide. Therefore, it could be called the unofficial continuing musical representative of the event. Entitled "Olympic Fanfare" or "Olympic Theme," it only took nine years to go from a section of a minor serious work to a media phenomenon. American Leo Arnaud (1904-), who otherwise is little known, wrote the parent piece "Charge!" in 1959. The fanfare was lifted from the "Bugler's Dream" portion of "Charge!", thus elevating a potentially obscure melody to the full glory of Olympic history.

Rock Around the Clock

Who would have guessed back in 1955 that the raucous recording by Bill Haley and the Comets was the start of a controversial new era in American popular music? Otherwise little-known songwriters Max C. Freedman and Jimmy DeKnight created the lively hard rhythm composition "Rock Around the Clock," which began it all in 1953. The next year, in 1954, the success of "Rock Around the Clock," which was not recorded until 1955, was followed by the similar style songs "Sh-Boom" by James Keyes, Claude and Carl Feaster, Floyd F. McRae, and James Edwards (five authors!) and "Shake, Rattle and Roll" by Charles Calhoun.

By the time "Rock Around the Clock" was used as the background music for the 1955 movie *The Blackboard Jungle*, the dam had begun to burst and rock and roll, for good or bad, became a substantial element in American, and eventually, international culture. In addition to being pioneers of the new musical form, the three songs mentioned above have quite interesting titles. The transition piece "Sh-Boom" semantically symbolized the shift from the gentler and quieter (but far from dull) music of the earlier period ("Sh") to the harsher and louder music of the later period ("Boom"). Although disc jockey Alan Freed technically first used the term "rock and roll" in 1951, in historical reality the extremely famous "Rock Around the Clock" gave the rock and roll era the first part of its name, and the also famous "Shake, Rattle and Roll" was the inspiration for the second part. Because of the ridiculously huge financial rewards of rock music, the "roll" term, on the other hand, could have been derived from the sizable rolls of money that were deposited in the bank.

Rocky Mountain High

There are a lot of highs connected with the 1972 ballad "Rocky Mountain High." The song went high in the pop charts, it was composed and performed by a young man who adopted the name of the mile high city, Denver, for his artistic career, and it was sung in a clear, high, soaring voice.

Furthermore, "Rocky Mountain High" was possibly the high point in the life of singer and composer John Denver (1943-). With good lyrics and an exhilarating melody capable of transporting us far above the peaks of the great mountain chain, "Rocky Mountain High" is most representative of the musical skills and philosophical outlook of Denver. That song, by Denver and Michael C. Taylor, plus "Take Me Home, Country Roads" (1971) by Denver and Bill and Taffy Danoff, as well as "Leaving on a Jet Plane" (1969) and "Annie's Song" (1974) by Denver alone, collectively comprise a significant departure from most popular music of the period.

Folkish and old-fashioned, somewhat like Simon and Garfunkel's 1967 "Scarborough Fair" and Paul Simon's 1970 solo effort "Bridge Over Troubled Water," Denver's sentimental compositions reflect his rural background, his ecologically oriented lifestyle, and his cherubic, boyish manner. Some persons might call him "square" and "dull." But the full round tones of his extraordinary voice projecting his extremely successful songs way up into the stratosphere is anything but dull. It is a very pleasant change to have a 1970s song with a "rock" association performed by someone who isn't stoned.

Stop! in the Name of Love

In the swing era of the 1930s, 1940s, and early 1950s, the most successful female vocal group in the world of popular music was the Andrews Sisters. The three Andrews Sisters were succeeded by the three McGuire Sisters who produced some hit recordings in the 1950s. Following them were the three Supremes, a trio of friends from Detroit, who were as dominant in the 1960s as the Andrews Sisters had been 20 years earlier.

With Diana Ross as the star of the winsome threesome along with Mary Wilson and Frances Ballard (later replaced by Cindy Birdsong), the Supremes found themselves number one in the pop charts ten times between 1964 and 1967. (By doing so, they greatly aided the financial success of the Motown label, their hometown recording company.) Three of their top hits were "Where Did Our Love Go?" (1964), "Baby Love" (1964), and "Stop! in the Name of Love" (1965). The latter song, composed by Eddie Holland, Lamont Dozier, and Brian Holland, is perhaps the most representative piece popularized by the group. (The Hollands and Dozier also wrote "Where Did Our Love Go?" and "Baby Love.")

In 1969, Diana Ross left the Supremes to follow a highly successful solo and film career. Since then, no other female singing ensemble has reigned supreme in popular music, thus breaking the several decade chain of terrific trios.

Tie a Yellow Ribbon 'Round the Ole Oak Tree

They say that timing is everything. So when you take a pleasant melody with good words that fit the mood of the moment, the chances for a song being a hit are greatly increased.

Irwin Levine and L. Russell Brown wrote the 1973 winner "Tie a Yellow Ribbon 'Round the Ole Oak Tree" to describe the sentiments of a man returning from incarceration in prison. The return of many thousands of military personnel from the much-despised Vietnam War at about the same time surely must have enhanced the public acceptance of the ballad. But the Vietnam veterans did not get the same kind of welcome home as did the GIs at the end of World War II. Many of them individually were greeted by warm, sincere, and enthusiastic homecomings similar to that given to the returnee in the song, but collectively the general societal reception in the U.S. was cool.

The hometown sweetheart in "Yellow Ribbon" immediately responded to the event by tying many yellow ribbons around the famous old oak. After a decade, the American public finally responded to the sacrifices of Vietnam by establishing a memorial in Washington. The color of the monument contrasted greatly with the loving yellow in the lively song. The stone war symbol is black.

Tom Dooley

There were two Tom Dooleys affiliated with the 1958 ballad "Tom Dooley." The first Tom Dooley, originally Tom Dula, was a North Carolina man sentenced to die for an 1866 murder he probably didn't commit. The second Tom Dooley (1927-1961) was a physician who helped treat thousands of refugees from North Vietnam in 1954. For this very magnaminous activity and other medical projects, plus his books describing his experiences, Dooley became world famous. He was like the Mother Teresa of the 1950s.

"Tom Dooley" the hit song was written about the first Tom, the supposed criminal. Dave Guard is credited with adapting it from a Blue Ridge Mountain folk piece, "Tom Dula," and the Kingston Trio popularized it. (There is some dispute over who converted it from the folk to the mainstream arena and when.)

But quite strangely Tom number two, the doctor, died of cancer not long after the song appeared, and the tragedy of the lyrics also somewhat applied to him. A few years following Dooley's premature death, the U.S. became involved in a bitter war in the very land where Dooley performed his medical acts of compassion. The ballad technically belongs to a much earlier time than the 1950s and 1960s, but it culturally and psychologically belongs to those decades.

Top of the World

They were on the top of the world when Karen prematurely died of an eating disorder. Golden-throated Karen Carpenter (1950-1983) and her talented brother Richard (1946-) were the darlings of soft, gentle, and reflective popular music during the 1970s and early 1980s.

Performing tender ballads such as "Close to You" (1970), "Rainy Days and Mondays" (1971), and "Top of the World" (1973), the Carpenters constructed a fine and beautiful musical structure of a very unique design. But it all fell apart with Karen's untimely demise.

Complementing their sweet duets (Karen was the prominent lead singer) were a series of good compositions, notably the above three. "Top of the World" was written by Richard Carpenter and John Bettis, and "Rainy Days" by Roger Nicholls and Paul Williams. "Close to You" was written by composer Burt Bacharach and lyricist Hal David. The 1970 "Close to You" should not be confused with the 1943 ballad "Close to You" by Al Hoffman, Carl G. Lampe, and Jerry Livingston.

Hoffman and Livingston, incidentally, also collaborated with Mack David on two songs for the 1950 Disney animated masterpiece *Cinderella*. Their sentimental "A Dream Is a Wish Your Heart Makes" possibly may have been suitable for Karen's pure, clear tones of honey, but "Bibbidi, Bobbidi, Boo's" bouncy gibberish was definitely not typical Carpenter material. Yet there is sort of a connection between the 1950 movie and Karen because of her musical rags-to-riches Cinderella story. Also, just as Cinderella had her glass slipper, Karen had her own personal house of glass which unfortunately cut short her wondrous and charming musical tale.

The Twist

The word "twist" takes many semantic twists. In one unabridged English language dictionary, no less than 49 variant usages of the word as a verb or noun are listed. Among the entries is one for a vigorous, gyrating, uninhibited, and free-wheeling dance performed by couples. That meaning of "twist" entered the dictionary after 1960, when young Chubby Checker popularized the song "The Twist" in a best-selling recording. For a while, "The Twist" was almost as big a dance craze as the Charleston had been in the 1920s.

The two dances had much in common. Legs, arms, and torsos swung wildly, the music was very energetic, the dancing was good exercise, and everybody had fun. The basic differences between the two was that the Charleston featured a jolting forward and back motion, as if an earthquake had struck, and the twist involved sort of a circular movement as if a tornado had arrived.

Chubby Checker became a well-known entertainment personality because of his promotion of "The Twist," but composer Hank Ballard, who wrote the song in 1958, is hardly known. That's a truly ironic historical twist.

Up Up and Away

Jim Webb was a directional composer. In 1967 he musically traveled to the Southwest with "By the Time I Get to Phoenix." A year later he was a lineman for a county in the Midwest with "Wichita Lineman." Then in 1969 he went all the way down to the Gulf of Mexico with "Galveston."

But his best trip via song involved going straight up into the atmosphere. "Up Up and Away," or, "My Beautiful Balloon," an airy, uplifting, high flying melodic voyage, was written in 1967 after his sweetheart had left his web and married another.

Assisted by an excellent recording utilizing the smooth tones of the Fifth Dimension, Webb received a Grammy Award for his balloon ballad. Incidentally, in addition to being a very pleasant vocal group, the Fifth Dimension has a most interesting name. Although devised to reflect the number of singers in the ensemble, another more esoteric possibility is suggested. We are all aware of the quite visible three physical dimensions as well as Einstein's theoretical fourth dimension of time. Could it be that there is yet another dimension in our existence, a fifth dimension, that consists of human individuality and creativity? Such an added dimension would go far to help explain much that has occurred through the long history of the world.

BROADWAY
1900-1939

Ah, Sweet Mystery of Life

Life was no big mystery for composer Victor Herbert. With his talent for writing fine works for the musical stage, the sweetness of fame and financial successful came to him in big doses. His two most famous theatrical productions were *Babes in Toyland*, a 1903 musical extravaganza that has become a favorite at Christmas, and *Naughty Marietta*, a 1910 operetta.

Babes in Toyland featured two famous songs, the sparkling instrumental "March of the Toys" and the beloved bit of nostalgia, "Toyland" (words by Glen MacDonough). *Naughty Marietta* did just as well. The score by Herbert (1859-1924) and lyricist Rida Johnson Young (1869-1926) contained three enduring songs, "I'm Falling in Love with Someone," "Tramp, Tramp, Tramp Along the Highway," and best of all, "Ah, Sweet Mystery of Life" (or "The Dream Melody"). With excellent words and a smooth, dreamlike, somewhat saccharine melody, "Mystery" is one of Herbert's most skillful compositions.

Yet considering Herbert's reputation and preeminence in the theater around the turn of the century, the above pieces plus a few others, like the comedic "Every Day Is Ladies' Day" (1906) written with Henry Blossom, comprise a surprisingly meager long-term legacy. Music for the stage is always vulnerable to the changing tastes of the public. Herbert like most others fell victim to the march of time just as generations have been captivated by his "March of the Toys."

Ain't Misbehavin'

In their jazz classic, Andy Razaf and "Fats" Waller made the claim "Ain't Misbehavin'." If that number from the 1929 revue *Hot Chocolates* was speaking the truth, it is difficult to discover what they did with their time, for they certainly did not write a lot of hit songs.

Composer Waller (1904-1943), whose real first name was Thomas, and lyricist Razaf (1895-1973) did co-produce another good perennial, "Honeysuckle Rose" (1929). Razaf also wrote the outstanding swing era favorite "In the Mood" (1939) with composer Joe Garland and a second set of lyrics for "Twelfth Street Rag" in 1942. The first lyric for "Rag" was written by James S. Sumner in 1919 to go with Euday L. Bowman's classic 1914 piano composition. (Incidentally, "Ain't Misbehavin'"'s co-composer Harry Brooks [1895-1970] did nothing else of consequence.)

Even granted that three of these pieces are very highly regarded, a legacy of one classic and one standard plus half of two other classics is not exactly an impressive output from two persons who supposedly were on their best behavior. Of course, many other persons also more or less stay within the limits of good conduct, but few even accomplish what Razaf and Waller did. So there should be no more off-the-wall razzing of this moderately productive and significant pair of artists.

All the Things You Are

Success often comes out of failure. After a series of hits, the final Broadway musical by Jerome Kern (1885-1945) was a flop. Though combining the talents of two of the biggest names in the history of the American stage, Kern and Oscar Hammerstein II (1895-1960), *Very Warm for May* (1939) just did not make it. However, it did leave behind one of the finest ballads of all time, "All the Things You Are."

Pensive and subtle, "All the Things" is a lovely listing of the various charms of the person being serenaded. Many of us have tried to express the sentiments of the lyrics to a sweetheart, normally with much less poetic skill. Few of us have tried to compose a melody to please our lover, and even fewer have succeeded in creating anything that in any way approached the appeal of Kern's exceptional melody.

The failure of *Very Warm for May* did nothing to slow down Kern and Hammerstein. One year later they collaborated on the Academy Award-winning song "The Last Time I Saw Paris," and three years after that, with the premiere of *Oklahoma!*, Hammerstein began his fantastic artistic partnership with Richard Rodgers. There is a kernel of an object lesson in this anecdote that should not have to be hammered home.

April in Paris

When it's April in Paris, with the natural beauties of spring further enhancing the manmade beauties of the city, one tends to walk a little slower. By sauntering instead of dashing the appreciation of the scenery and the atmosphere is absorbed even more fully. Yet when the lovely nostalgic ballad "April in Paris" was first introduced in a 1932 revue, what was the name of the show? Very inappropriately, it was *Walk a Little Faster.*

Possibly that incongruity was one of the factors that delayed widespread recognition of the song's merits. No matter, for eventually the delicate tribute to the delicate metropolis caught on and became a perennial standard. The words by Edgar Yipsel Harburg (1898-1981) and the melody by Vernon Duke (1903-1969) blend together so well that it is surprising to discover that this was their only joint hit. Harburg had a few other big winners with other composers including the Irish-flavored favorite "How Are Things in Glocca Mora?" (1947) with Burton Lane, the magic-flavored classic "Over the Rainbow" (1939) with Harold Arlen, and the outer space-flavored "Adrift on a Star" ("Here we are, adrift on a star"), a set of dreamy lyrics set to Jacques Offenbach's famous 1881 "Barcarolle."

Duke (born Vladimir Dukelsky in Russia) also worked successfully with other lyricists. He produced "Taking a Chance on Love" (1940) with John Latouche and Ted Fetter, and "Autumn in New York" (1934) with himself as collaborator. The latter song came three years after "April in Paris," which still at that time had gained little attention. Apparently Duke tried another season and another city when "April" had not taken off. It would be fascinating to speculate which communities he would have linked with summer and winter if both his spring and autumn ballads had flopped.

Begin the Beguine

Before there was Nat "King" Cole, the splendid velvet-voiced vocalist, there was "king" Cole Porter, one of the rulers of Broadway. Porter (1891-1964) created the words and music for a number of well-known shows, including *Anything Goes* (1934), *Kiss Me Kate* (1948), and *Can-Can* (1953).

These and other Broadway and Hollywood musicals produced an abundance of standard songs. In the 1920s and 1930s there were "You Do Something to Me" (1929), "What Is This Thing Called Love?" (1929), "Night and Day" (1932), "Anything Goes" (1934), "Blow, Gabriel, Blow" (1934), "I Get a Kick Out of You" (1934), "It's De-Lovely" (1936), "You're the Top" (1934), "Begin the Beguine" (1935), "Just One of Those Things" (1935), "I've Got You Under My Skin" (1936), "From Now On" (1938), and "My Heart Belongs to Daddy" (1938). In the 1940s and 1950s, there were "You'd Be So Nice to Come Home To" (1942), "Another Op'nin', Another Show" (1948), "So In Love" (1948), "Why Can't You Behave?" (1948), "Wunderbar" (1948), "Be a Clown" (1948), "From This Moment On" (1950), "I Love Paris" (1953), and "True Love" (1956).

One of the more unique Cole Porter compositions is "Begin the Beguine," a classic introduced in the 1935 musical *Jubilee* along with "Just One of the Those Things." "Beguine" almost became one of those things that are presented in a show and then forgotten. Possibly because the public generally did not know that the beguine is a South American bolero-style dance, and possibly because of the song's unusual length, "Beguine" did not catch on until Artie Shaw made a top-selling instrumental recording in 1938. Then all America began the beguine.

The Best Things in Life Are Free

It follows logically that if the best things in life are free, then the worst things require cash. So therefore food, clothing, housing, medical care, and other things that we regard as necessities must be in the category of worst things.

This shows how "logic," like statistics, can be twisted to any purpose. The 1927 song "The Best Things in Life Are Free" is simply trying to elicit appreciation for stars, the moon, flowers, birds, and other aspects of nature as mutually sharable, cost-free counterbalances to the dubious values of man-made diversions. The piece could be cynically looked at as a little puff of Pollyanna, but it could also be optimistically interpreted as being very similar in spirit to the 1948 novelty "Enjoy Yourself, It's Later Than You Think." This song, with words by Herb Magidson and music by Carl Sigman, is, like the other composition, a statement that we should stop once in awhile and contact the commonly available simple pleasures of life.

The creators of "Best Things" were the highly successful team of songwriters, lyricists Bud De Sylva (1895-1950) and Lew Brown (1893-1958) and composer Ray Henderson (1896-1971). In addition to "Best Things," which was written for the musical *Good News*, the trio produced "The Birth of the Blues" (1926), "It All Depends on You" (1926), "The Varsity Drag" (1927), "Button Up Your Overcoat" (1928), "You're the Cream in My Coffee" (1928), and "Sunny Side Up" or "Keep Your Sunny Side Up" (1929).

De Sylva, Brown, and Henderson also worked with other collaborators. De Sylva wrote "April Showers" (1921) to a tune by Louis Silvers, "California, Here I Come" (1924) with Al Jolson to a tune by Joseph Meyer, "If You Knew Susie" (1925) to another tune by Meyer, and "You're an Old Smoothie" (1932) to a tune by Richard A. Whiting and Nacio Herb Brown. Lew Brown wrote "That Old Feeling" (1937) to a tune by Sammy Fain, "Don't Sit Under the

Apple Tree" (1939) with Charles Tobias to a tune by Sam H. Stept, and the English lyrics (1939) to "Beer Barrel Polka." Henderson wrote the melodies for "That Old Gang of Mine" (1923) to go with words by Billy Rose and Mort Dixon, "Alabamy Bound" (1925) to go with words by Bud De Sylva and Bud Green, "Five Foot Two, Eyes of Blue" (1925) and "I'm Sitting on Top of the World" (1925) to go with words by Sam M. Lewis and Joe Young, and "Bye, Bye, Blackbird" (1926) to go with words by Mort Dixon.

This long list of good popular compositions by De Sylva, Brown, and Henderson tends to support the sentiments of "The Best Things in Life Are Free." After all these songs and countless others are available to use gratis via radio, television, free concerts, and our own memories.

The Birth of the Blues

One of the scandals of 1926 was associated with George White. It wasn't a political scandal involving the White House or a congressman publicly imbibing too much white lightning. Instead, it was a musical scandal on the great White Way, also known as Broadway.

George White's Scandals of 1926, a lively annual revue, turned white into blue. Lyricists Bud De Sylva (1895-1950) and Lew Brown (1893-1958) and composer Ray Henderson (1896-1971) wrote the blues classic "The Birth of the Blues" specifically for the show. The songwriting team of course did not personally witness the birth (or better evolution) of that particular form of black jazz, since it probably occurred some time before they were born and in locales hidden from the mainstream cultural environment. They were old enough, however, to witness the widespread popularizing of the blues after 1910. Most importantly, they devised an imaginative and artistically excellent musical description of how the blues might have come into existence. Their composition also was a most colorful piece, with white, black, blue, brown, and silver (Sylva) affecting the song.

"The Birth of the Blues" was one of the best-known songs to be introduced in one of the *George White's Scandals*, which were produced from 1919 to 1939 with several years skipped. "Life Is Just a Bowl of Cherries," with words by Brown and music by Henderson, brought the color red to the 1931 *Scandals*. In the 1924 *Scandals*, De Sylva and Ballard MacDonald collaborated on the words for the classic "Somebody Loves Me" to go with George Gershwin's melody. What color love represents, though, is still being debated.

Charleston

The word "Charleston" is associated with two periods of turmoil in U.S. history. In 1861, the shots that precipitated the tumultuous Civil War were fired in Charleston, South Carolina. In 1923, the song that precipitated the biggest and most scandalous dance craze in American history was introduced in the revue *Runnin' Wild*. For several years after that the "Charleston" ran wild and did as much as anything to contribute to the roar of the roaring '20s. With a lively, jerky melody and dance steps that made the later physical conditioning craze of aerobics seem like a nap, the "Charleston" was not only a lot of fun but it helped keep you slim and healthy.

Written by Cecil Mack (1883-1944) and Jimmy Johnson, the "Charleston" made such an impact on U.S. culture that a generation later it was resurrected in not one but two excellent motion pictures. In *Tea for Two* (1950), "Charleston" was a featured production number. In the classic 1946 Christmas movie *It's a Wonderful Life*, Jimmy Stewart and Donna Reed unintentionally ended up in a swimming pool while trying the "Charleston" for the first time. Soon the wet couple were joined by the rest of the dancers who, swept up by the excitement of the dance's frantic combination of running in place and wild swinging of arms, intentionally jumped into the water. The scene was happy chaos–the normal reaction to the "Charleston."

Dancing in the Dark

One of the essential ingredients for a successful song is to fully transmit the mood of the subject. The old standard "Dancing in the Dark" does just that. Slow, sensuous, mystical, and muted, with a definite impression of tenativeness and anticipation, "Dancing" is a superb representation of two close together lovers passionately moving around a dance floor. No other American popular song has as capably captured the blend of dance, trance, and romance.

Introduced in the 1931 revue *The Band Wagon*, "Dancing" is the best-known composition by Howard Dietz and Arthur Schwartz. (Somehow the subdued atmosphere of "Dancing" and the brash image of a band wagon just don't go together.) Lyricist Dietz (1896-1983) and composer Schwartz (1900-1984) also produced "Something to Remember You By" (1930), "You and the Night and the Music" (1934), "That's Entertainment" (1953), and others. Their principal effort, though, was the mini-masterpiece "Dancing."

If the puritanical censors were in power then, one of their targets might be "Dancing in the Dark." In this case such censorship would not be due to the words, but the implied eroticism of the melody. Whether or not this characteristic was consciously intended, Schwartz certainly did his part in making "Dancing" a tremendous commercial and artistic success.

The Desert Song

Hungarian-born Sigmund Romberg (1887-1951) was one of the most prominent composers of the U.S. musical theater. His Viennese style works, notably the trio of outstanding operettas, *The Student Prince* (1924), *The Desert Song* (1926), and *New Moon* (1928), made him one of the big names of his era.

The Desert Song, a tale of romance in the desolate wastes of Morocco, contained two fine love numbers written with the then young but in time great lyricist Oscar Hammerstein II (1895-1960) and the respected established wordsmith Otto Harbach (1873-1963). The wistful "One Alone" and the extraordinary and mystical title song, also known as "Blue Heaven," were the musical stars of the show. In case you have never heard the haunting strains of "The Desert Song," it is well worth hunting for a recording of the song.

"Desert Song" is quite possibly Romberg's best composition. "Drinking Song" from *The Student Prince*, "Lover, Come Back to Me" and "Stout-Hearted Men" from *New Moon*, and the graceful sentimental waltz "When I Grow Too Old to Dream," created with Hammerstein for the 1935 movie *The Night Is Young*, are excellent too. And we shouldn't forget "Will You Remember?" or "Sweetheart" (from the 1917 operetta *Maytime*), whose very familiar waltz melody and "Sweetheart, sweetheart, sweetheart" lyrics by Rida Johnson Young are still remembered well. But "The Desert Song" is one of a kind–a unique esthetic experience.

Drinking Song

The rousing "Drinking Song" from *The Student Prince* (1924) is sort of a cross between "Drink to Me Only with Thine Eyes" and "There Is a Tavern in the Town." It has some of the tender romance of "Drink to Me," the 1616 love poem by Ben Jonson that was linked with an anonymous English tune in the late eighteenth century. It has all of the exuberance and abandon of the anonymous late nineteenth century American phenomenon "Tavern in the Town."

In other words, it is a superlative composition. "Drinking Song" (or "Drink, Drink, Drink") is the key number of *The Student Prince* and is a main reason for the show's continuing performance by amateur theater groups. A good plot and a fine supporting cast of songs also helped to make the operetta the most famous creation of composer Sigmund Romberg (1887-1951).

The best of the other songs were the romantic duet "Deep in My Heart," the nostalgic duet "Golden Days," and "Serenade" ("Overhead the moon is beaming"), the prince's pledge of love. All of these four pieces had melodies that were richer in texture and more substantial than most operetta compositions of the era.

They also had very good lyrics by Dorothy Donnelly (1880-1928) as indicated by the subtle blend of romance and humor in "Drinking Song's" familiar lines "Here's a hope that those bright eyes will shine, longingly, lovingly, soon into mine." In her lyrics, Donnelly skillfully brought together dear, cheer, and beer.

Give My Regards to Broadway

"Give My Regards to Broadway" sounds like the song of a stage veteran, but it was just the opposite. It was one of the two top pieces that in 1904 introduced young George M. Cohan (1878-1942) as a successful composer and performer into the Broadway scene. In his musical *Little Johnny Jones*, Cohan confidently strode into the hearts of America with "Give My Regards" and "Yankee Doodle Boy."

A series of subsequent shows completely established Cohan as the darling of the New York theater world, and left us with several more enduring songs. *Forty-five Minutes from Broadway* (1906) had the title song and "Mary's a Grand Old Name." *George Washington, Jr.* (1906) featured the outstanding patriotic favorite "You're a Grand Old Flag." And *Fifty Miles from Boston* (1908) brought "Harrigan" to the public.

By the time he had written "Over There" (1917), the leading musical symbol of U.S. involvement in World War I and Cohan's best song away from the theatrical footlights, he had been the most dominant figure on Broadway for more than a decade. But soon after that, writer, producer, composer, actor, singer, and personality Cohan began to fade, mostly because his old-fashioned creations found less and less favor with audiences. Although Cohan is not generally regarded as a great artist, he gave the theater of his time a brash shot in the arm. With his legacy of four strong classics, "Give My Regards," "Yankee Doodle Boy," "Over There," and "Grand Old Flag," he is one of the foremost popular composers of the first two decades of the century.

I Got Rhythm

Rhythm is one of the more important things in life. Rhythm in nature, for instance biological cycles, is essential. Rhythm at work, for instance assembly lines, is necessary. Rhythm in sports, for instance a golf swing, is vital for top performance. And rhythm in the arts, notably poetry and music, gives them much of their identity.

Two artists that had rhythm were the Gershwin brothers. George (1898-1937) was, arguably, the best American composer of all time, creating several fine classical masterpieces plus a number of top popular songs. Ira (1896-1983), George's almost constant collaborator, was an author of many excellent lyrics. That is why they were completely unafraid to proclaim their skill in the famous song "I Got Rhythm."

"Rhythm" originally didn't have rhythm. When George first wrote the melody, it had a slow and ineffective tempo. Several years after the tune was put aside, it was resurrected, speeded up, given more vitality, and inserted in the 1930 show *Girl Crazy*. Accompanied by Ira's clever words, including the famous line "Who can ask for anything more?," the song, as well as the show, became a big hits.

Although "I Got Rhythm" didn't need much help to make *Girl Crazy* a success, it got it. Assisting in the success was the good standard "Bidin' My Time" and the very good standard "But Not for Me." But even more beneficial to the production was the splendid love classic, "Embraceable You." That ballad would surely have been the hit of the show if "I Got Rhythm" hadn't preempted that role. Indeed, it is quite unusual to have two pop masterpieces in one Broadway show, but it happened in *Girl Crazy*. Who can ask for anything more?

Indian Love Call

They call it "Indian Love Call," but because of its loud somewhat untamed almost screeching strains, cynics could easily describe it as the mating call of the wild Canadian moose. The operetta from which it comes, *Rose Marie* (1924), is appropriately set in the Canadian Rockies with Mounties, murder, love, and all. (From the volume of the lines "When I'm calling you, oo-oo-oo-oo-oo-oo!" the song could be from the murder scene, too.)

Despite "Love Call's" peculiarities and vulnerability to being the target of jokes and satire, it has become a quaint standard over the years. Popularized by Jeanette MacDonald and Nelson Eddy in a 1936 best-selling record, the love duet came to be the calling card of the two singers and their most famous performance. A generation after its introduction, "Love Call" was reportedly the favorite of President Dwight Eisenhower. Who would have guessed that the quiet man who so calmly led Allied forces in World War II and who was the stable chief executive of the United States in the domestically docile 1950s would be so attached to this bellicose tribute to bellowing?

MacDonald, Eddy, and Eisenhower weren't the only celebrities connected with "Love Call." Its creators were the very successful composer Rudolf Friml (1879-1972) and the outstanding lyricists Otto Harbach (1873-1963) and Oscar Hammerstein II (1895-1960). Hammerstein would become most famous by his later association with Richard Rodgers, with whom he never collaborated on anything resembling a moose call.

Look for the Silver Lining

"Look for the Silver Lining" is by no means the best creation of composer Jerome Kern (1885-1945). "Smoke Gets in Your Eyes" (1933), "The Last Time I Saw Paris" (1940), and especially "Ol' Man River" (1927) are probably superior compositions. In some ways though, "Silver Lining" was most typical of the smooth and polished talents of the fine song writer. One of Kern's earliest hits, from the 1920 musical *Sally*, it represents in mood and style the essence of the musician–excellent artistry, a certain degree of depth, and a generally upbeat life. Nobody less than Judy Garland sang "Silver Lining" in the 1946 film biography of Kern, *Till the Clouds Roll By*, and Garland's rendition was one of the main features of the movie.

The third human component in the history of "Silver Lining" was Bud (George) De Sylva (1895-1950), the author of the uplifting words. De Sylva had a habit of writing successful lyrics with a positive tone. "April Showers" (1921), "California Here I Come" (1924), and the "Best Things in Life Are Free" (1927) all displayed a happy face. Even when the theme was the blues, i.e., "The Birth of the Blues" (1926), the attitude was friendly and lively. So it appears that De Sylva, at least in his professional work, usually looked for the "sylva" lining.

Manhattan

Manhattan is the best-known of the five boroughs of New York City. The 1925 ballad "Manhattan" is the best-composed of the three famous songs about "the big apple." "The Sidewalks of New York" (1894) by James W. Blake and Charles B. Lawlor is the oldest and most famous of the trio, and "New York, New York" (1944), with music by Leonard Bernstein and words by Betty Comden and Adolph Green, is also a very good song.

Artistically though, smooth, romantic "Manhattan" rises above the other pieces in the same manner as that borough's skyline dominates the rest of the metropolis. The melody was by Richard Rodgers (1902-1979), who was a most dominating figure on the skyline of twentieth century music. The lyrics were by Lorenz Hart (1895-1943), the first of Rodger's two outstanding collaborators. Their composition, which was introduced in the revue *The Garrick Gaieties*, was, along with the similar style "Bewitched, Bothered and Bewildered" (1940), among the songwriting team's very best.

Despite the title, "Manhattan" is really a love song for the entire city as is evident from the references to "the Bronx and Staten Island too." Like the common outsider image of Manhattan (particularly mid-town) being the true New York City, "Manhattan's" title does give somewhat of a false impression. But what else can you expect from a community long connected with flim-flam, beginning with the first financial dealings between Peter Minuit and the local Indians.

The Most Beautiful Girl in the World

Waltzes are most usually associated with the nineteenth and the early twentieth centuries. The Strausses of Vienna, Franz Lehár of "Merry Widow" fame, Peter Ilich Tchaikovsky, the great Russian composer, and others were masters of this so elegant 3/4 time art form.

The most eloquent exponent of the waltz in the middle part of the twentieth century was, perhaps, Richard Rodgers. The great musicals that Rodgers (1902-1979) created with Oscar Hammerstein II are frequently graced with waltz tempo pieces. "Oh, What a Beautiful Mornin'" from *Oklahoma* (1943) and the "Carousel Waltz" from *Carousel* (1945) are, for example, waltzes in the finest traditions of Vienna.

The lesser-known Rodgers musicals also sometimes feature waltz style numbers. For *State Fair*, a moderately successful 1945 movie (remade in 1962), Rodgers and Hammerstein conceived a waltz rouser, "It's a Grand Night for Singing." After Hammerstein's death, Rodgers created both words and music for the slow, pensive waltz "The Sweetest Sounds" in the 1962 musical *No Strings*. But before he teamed with Hammerstein, he collaborated with Lorenz Hart (1895-1943) on several waltz-containing musicals. The best 3/4 rhythm pieces by them are probably the lilting "Falling in Love with Love" from *The Boys from Syracuse* (1938) and "The Most Beautiful Girl in the World" from *Jumbo* (1935).

Rodgers wrote so many good waltzes that he easily could be adopted into the Strauss family. But then he would be called "Richard Strauss" and that name has already been preempted by the famous German classical composer. The bizarre music of Richard the German clashes with the polished compositions of Richard the American and his adopted Viennese cousins. So if the matter of changing names ever came up, Rodgers would from the afterlife have to reply, "No thanks for the honor."

My Funny Valentine

Rodgers and Hart missed Valentine's Day by two months. Their musical *Babes in Arms*, which featured "My Funny Valentine," opened on the 14th of the month, but not in February. It was on *April* 14, 1937, that this show with Richard Rodgers' and Lorenz Hart's best collaborative score ever premiered on Broadway.

In addition to the wistful "My Funny Valentine," the show contained four other standard songs. The brash and brazen "The Lady Is a Tramp" was a definite attention getter. (The title of this piece could have inspired the name for the 1955 Walt Disney animated cartoon classic, *Lady and the Tramp*.) Add to these the two fine love ballads "Where or When?" and "I Wish I Were in Love Again" plus the vigorous and unique novelty "Johnny One Note," and you have a most note-able show.

Other musicals by Rodgers (1902-1979) and Hart (1895-1943) produced "Manhattan" (1925), "Mountain Greenery" (1926), "Thou Swell" (1927), "With a Song in My Heart" (1929), "Lover" (1933), "The Most Beautiful Girl in the World" (1935), "There's a Small Hotel" (1936), "Falling in Love with Love" (1938), "I Married an Angel" (1938), "Spring Is Here" (1938), "This Can't Be Love" (1938), and "Bewitched, Bothered and Bewildered" (1940). But *Babes in Arms*, just one of over two dozen Rodgers and Hart productions, contributed more than its share of fine music.

A footnote should be made here. Although Rodgers usually was quite original, the tune for "My Funny Valentine" may have been partially borrowed from Tchaikovsky's great 1890 ballet *The Sleeping Beauty*. Another well-known popular song also possibly influenced by the ballet was "I Wonder Who's Kissing Her Now" (1909). Joseph E. Howard and Harold Orlob are both credited with the melody of "I Wonder," while Will M. Hough and Frank R. Adams did the lyrics.

Night and Day

Sometimes a number from a musical becomes so dominating that it overwhelms the rest of the show or so popular that its production of origin seems unimportant. Both apply to "Night and Day," perhaps the best song by the eminent composer Cole Porter (1891-1964).

In fact, Porter's 1932 musical *Gay Divorce* was dubbed as the "Night and Day Show." While "Night and Day" remains one of the strongest popular classics of all time, *Gay Divorce* has been more or less forgotten. The show's 1934 motion picture adaption, with the subtle title change to *The Gay Divorcée*, has also been relegated to the status of a relative obscurity in spite of the presence of "Night and Day" and another good song, "The Continental."

The latter piece, which was introduced in the film, may possibly have been named in jest after its composer Con Conrad. (The lyricist was Herb Magidson). Conrad also was involved with "Margie" (1920), for which he and J. Russel Robinson wrote the tune to go with Benny Davis' lyrics, "Ma, He's Making Eyes at Me" (1921) with lyricist Sidney Clare, and "Barney Google" (1923) with lyricist Billy Rose.

The combination of "The Continental" and "Night and Day" made the score of *The Gay Divorcée* an exceptional one. "Night and Day," with its moody, pulsating melody and intense lyrics, is the more outstanding of the two, of course, but "The Continental" is a fine, polished dance number. Incidentally, Porter got the inspiration for "Night and Day"'s melody from a native tune in Morocco, which is located on a far away continent(al).

Oh, How I Hate to Get Up in the Morning

Perhaps Irving Berlin (1888-1989) really hated to get up in the morning. But what he accomplished after he arose was simply phenomenal. He wrote the words and music for so many fine and even great songs that he has to be considered as a pop music genius, the supreme potentate of American popular music.

A partial list of his hits and standards would include "Alexander's Ragtime Band" (1911), "Always" (1925), "Blue Skies" (1927), "Cheek to Cheek" (1935), "Count Your Blessings" (1952), "Doin' What Comes Natur'lly" (1946), "Easter Parade" (1933), "Everybody's Doin' It" (1911), "The Girl that I Marry" (1946), "God Bless America" (1939), "Happy Holiday" (1942), "Heat Wave" (1933), "How Deep Is the Ocean" (1932), "It's a Lovely Day Today" (1950), "I've Got My Love to Keep Me Warm" (1937), "Let's Have Another Cup o' Coffee" (1932), "Let's Take an Old Fashioned Walk" (1948), "Oh, How I Hate to Get Up in the Morning" (1918), "A Pretty Girl Is Like a Melody" (1919), "Puttin' on the Ritz" (1929), "Remember" (1925), "Say It with Music" (1921), "Show Business" (1946), "Sun in the Morning" (1946), "They Say It's Wonderful" (1946), "This Is the Army Mr. Jones" (1942), "What'll I Do?" (1924), "White Christmas" (1942), "Woodman, Woodman, Spare that Tree" (1911), and "You Can't Get a Man with a Gun" (1946).

"Oh, How I Hate to Get Up in the Morning" and "This Is the Army Mr. Jones" were perhaps the most fun for Berlin. The first song was written for an all-soldier revue, *Yip, Yip, Yaphank*, during World War I with Berlin introducing the number. The second song was created for another all-soldier revue, *This Is the Army*, during World War II with the maestro again appearing in the show. In the World War II extravaganza, Berlin did not sing any of the new songs but instead reprieved "Oh, How I Hate to Get Up in the Morning," with its threat to murder the bugler, to the delight of a new generation.

Ol' Man River

The showpiece of the 1927 musical *Showboat*, "Ol' Man River," may well be the most significant song ever included in a Broadway musical. Dramatic, thought-provoking, sad, and beautiful, it certainly is one of the more poignant compositions in the history of the American theater. It also is one of the finest vehicles for the display of a deep, resonant male voice. All this plus a subtle but definite message of social consciousness decades before such trends were fashionable come together to make a true masterpiece of popular music.

The creators of "Ol' Man River" were two outstanding giants of Broadway. Jerome Kern (1885-1945) was then at the peak of his career, having already produced hits like "They Didn't Believe Me" (1914) with lyricist Michael E. Rourke. Oscar Hammerstein II (1895-1960) would still be in top form, with collaborator Richard Rodgers, 30 years later. Their collective inspiration, *Showboat*, was perhaps the dominant production of the 1920s. Not only did it have excellent music, including the numbers "Only Make Believe," "Can't Help Lovin' Dat Man," and "Why Do I Love You," it had more depth and dimension than its predecessors. The frothiness and shallowness, which were the general pattern in previous musicals, was replaced by substance and authenticity.

Showboat, although somewhat dated, is still revived for new generations. Eventually it will, like all such productions, fade away. But "Ol' Man River" may just keep rolling along like the mighty Mississippi it extols. It has outlasted by a number of years its creators, Kern and Hammerstein, and also Winston Churchill who quoted from the song in an early World War II speech. It has a strong chance of outlasting all who read these written lines. It will never survive beyond the life of the long river with the long name, of course. But if any popular song has the wherewithal to surpass the longevity of most other man-made enterprises, it would be "Ol' Man River."

A Pretty Girl Is Like a Melody

The unofficial second national anthem, the unofficial national Christmas carol, the unofficial national popular Easter song, and the unofficial anthem of the American theater–these were apparently not enough for pop genius Irving Berlin. On top of "God Bless America" (1939), "White Christmas" (1942), "Easter Parade" (1933), and "Show Business" (or "There's No Business Like Show Business") (1946), Berlin (1888-1989) also had to create "A Pretty Girl Is Like a Melody."

Written for the *Ziegfeld Follies of 1919*, "Pretty Girl" soon became the official theme of the "Follies" and its abundance of attractive women as well as the official or unofficial song of countless beauty contests and fashion shows around the world. (The most famous beauty pageant, though, has its own specially-created song. "Miss America" (1954), by Bernie Wayne, is the official theme of that annual contest.) So many pieces have been composed to describe the physical attributes of the female, but none have so overwhelmingly become the musical stereotype of womanly charms.

With so many fine songs flowing from Berlin's personable pen, it can be said that "Pretty Girl," in one way, wraps up the artist's attitude toward his music. By his achievements he declared, in effect, "A pretty tune is like a lovely girl." Yet beautiful women are far more common than the beauty-producing talents of sensitive musicians like Irving the Great.

’S Wonderful

Have you ever wondered why Ira Gershwin added an “S” in front of “wonderful” in the 1927 song “ ’S Wonderful?” Why not use just “Wonderful,” which does not change the beat at all, or “It’s wonderful” and slightly alter the tempo? Possibly Ira (1896-1983) felt the strange extra letter would add interest and be an attention getter, which was true. Or possibly he had an unconscious urge to create yet another George Gershwin classic beginning with “S.”

No matter what the motivation may have been, the effect was to supply one more to the unusually disproportionate number of exceptional Gershwin pieces starting with that letter. On top of “ ’S Wonderful,” there were “Somebody Loves Me,” “Someone to Watch Over Me,” “Strike Up the Band,” “Summertime,” and “Swanee.” These six alone would have made successful careers for most composers, but George Gershwin (1898-1937) was so much more than most composers.

Speaking of repeating letters, the 1927 musical in which “ ’S Wonderful” first appeared also played that same kind of alphabet game. The show’s letter was not “S,” or “G” like the three starting the names of the composer and lyricist, but “F” like in *Funny Face*, starring facile-footed Fred Astaire.

September Song

When a song has a bold declaratory title like "September Song," as if there were no others inspired by that lovely month, it better be good. Inherent in such a name is a suggestion of laying exclusive claim to the first part of autumn, so the fulfillment of the implied promise must be completely satisfactory. A similar situation, the 1946 classic "The Christmas Song" (or "Chestnuts Roasting on an Open Fire") by Mel Tormé and Robert Wells, makes an even bolder statement by the usage of the elitist word "the."

Yet "The Christmas Song" is fully worthy of its high-reaching title, as is its earlier cousin, "September Song." Written in 1938 for the musical *Knickerbocker Holiday,* "September" is one of the very finest and most polished love ballads in American music history. The dreamy "But its a long, long while from May to December" lyrics were by the outstanding playwright Maxwell Anderson (1888-1959). He also penned the well-known dramas *Elizabeth the Queen* (1930), *Winterset* (1935), *Key Largo* (1939), and *Anne of the Thousand Days* (1948).

The music was by the German-born, later naturalized, American composer Kurt Weill (1900-1950). The style of the melody was designed to fit the limited vocal ability of actor Walter Huston, who introduced the ballad in *Knickerbocker Holiday.* Ironically, the tune created to accommodate a less-than-beautiful singing voice has become one of the most beautiful melodic expressions of romance. Another irony is that this tender and sentimental composition is so drastically different in mood from the other song for which Weill is famous, the violent but very attractive 1954 curiosity "Mack the Knife."

Smoke Gets in Your Eyes

Nowadays cigarette smoke in one's eyes is often a cause for confrontation between the smoker and non-smoker. But in 1933 when author Otto Harbach (1873-1963) and composer Jerome Kern (1885-1945) collaborated on the outstanding musical *Roberta*, "Smoke Gets in Your Eyes" was a show-stopping love song. Almost by itself, "Smoke" made the show flame into fame.

Roberta, the best of Harbach's and Kern's several joint projects, also indirectly brought about two other standards. In the 1935 screen version of *Roberta*, a pair of other songs were added to the production. "I Won't Dance," with music by Kern and lyrics by Harbach and Oscar Hammerstein II, and "Lovely to Look At," with music by Kern and words by Dorothy Fields and Jimmy McHugh, considerably enhanced the already excellent original Broadway score.

Supplemented by these two new songs, the movie *Roberta* presented an intriguing trio of romantic ballads that provided a nice little scenario for a love story. The fellow encounters a gal who is quite "Lovely to Look At," asks her to dance, and gets rejected initially by the curt response "I Won't Dance." Finally through persistence he gets her to change her mind. Soon both are caught up in the exquisitely seductive strains of "Smoke Gets in Your Eyes" while slowly traversing the dance floor. The plot is finished off by any of a thousand possible love songs, including "Who" *(*"Took My Heart Away"*)* (1925), another collaboration by Kern, Harbach, and Hammerstein, "The Way You Look Tonight" (1936), another link between Kern and Fields, or "I'm in the Mood for Love" (1935), another joint effort by Fields (lyricist) and McHugh (composer).

Somebody Loves Me

Song titles cannot be copyrighted, and generally that is a very good policy. Sometimes, though, it can create confusion. For example, there are two songs entitled "Somebody Loves Me." The first came in 1892 and was written by Hattie Starr, the first successful woman pop composer in America. The second, and much more famous one, came in the 1924 edition of the *George White's Scandals*.

The authors of the later piece were the fabulous musician George Gershwin (1898-1937) and lyricists Bud De Sylva (1895-1950) and Ballard MacDonald (1882-1935). (De Sylva wrote many other successful lyrics, and MacDonald also wrote the words for "The Trail of the Lonesome Pine" (1913) with composer Harry Carroll.)

To complicate the picture even more, a movie with the somewhat misleading name *Somebody Loves Me* appeared in 1952. It did include Gershwin's pensive love ballad, but that was the only Gershwin piece in the film. Several other standards also were presented, including "Smiles," "The Wang, Wang Blues," and "'Way Down Yonder in New Orleans." "Smiles" (1917) was created by lyricist J. Will Callahan and composer Lee S. Roberts. "Wang" (1921) was the joint effort of lyricists Gus Mueller and "Buster" Johnson and composer Henry Busse. "'Way Down Yonder" (1922) was written by lyricist Henry Creamer and composer J. Turner Layton.

A passing word should be said about the series of revues called *The Passing Show*. Running from 1912 through 1924, the extravaganzas introduced several well-known numbers, including the above-mentioned "Smiles," "Pretty Baby" (1916), words by Gus Kahn and music by Tony Jackson and Egbert Van Alstyne, and "I'm Forever Blowing Bubbles" (1918), words by James Kendis, James Brockman, and Nat Vincent and music by John William Kellette. *The Passing Shows* were a rival to the *Ziegfield Follies* (1907-1931, with three years missing) and *George White's Scandals* (1919-1939, with several years missing). Note that we are back to where we started.

Someone to Watch Over Me

Some people have said that actor, governor, and President Ronald Reagan had a charmed life. He was called "the teflon president" who came out right side up no matter what kind of crisis might develop. If these labels are true, the explanation for it all may be in the 1949 motion picture *John Loves Mary*. The hero and heroine declared as "our song" the recurring theme of the film. That theme was "Someone to Watch Over Me," and the hero was none other than Ronald Reagan.

Whether or not you read something theological or philosophical into this set of circumstances, it is certain that someone was watching over George Gershwin (1898-1937) during his abbreviated stay on earth. Perhaps the greatest of all American composers, Gershwin, usually with his also highly talented brother Ira (1896-1983), produced a long list of fine compositions.

"Someone to Watch Over Me" (1926) came at the height of Gershwin's career. His jazz masterpiece "Rhapsody in Blue" was created two years before in 1924, his also outstanding "Concerto in F" for piano was written just one year before in 1925, and his classic "An American in Paris" would be conceived two years later in 1928. "Someone to Watch," with lyrics by Ira, was the main number of the musical *Oh, Kay!*, which proved to be a lot more than just okay.

Song of the Vagabonds

It is relatively easy to remember the most famous songs of the renowned Czechoslovak-American operetta composer Rudolf Friml (1879-1972). Just remember "Indian Love Call" (who can forget that title or the song itself if you've heard it), and his three most famous stage works. *Firefly* (1912) showcased "Love Is Like a Firefly;" the ballad "Rose Marie" was the title piece of *Rose Marie* (1924); and the "Song of the Vagabonds" was the rousing centerpiece of *The Vagabond King* (1925). Isn't it handy to have the key words of these three compositions prominently sticking out in the show titles?

Not only has the recall of the name "Song of the Vagabonds" been made simpler by the course of history, but it is also hard to forget the song itself. What other piece starts out with anything resembling the startling lines "Sons of toil and danger, Will you serve a stranger?" (These lyrics, and those of "Only a Rose," also from the same operetta, are the best-known words by Brian Hooker (1880-1946)). How many other tunes have as much dynamism, drama, and volume? "Song of the Vagabonds" may not be to your taste, but it certainly cannot be described as modest, boring, or easy to ignore.

With its fervent and uninhibited call to fight against Burgundy, it is one of the more unique songs of the twentieth century. The "Burgundy" referred to, incidentally, is not the variety of wine but the region in eastern France that was a major power in the fifteenth century. The might of medieval Burgundy has long since vanished, but it has left behind in its historical wake the mighty good and mighty powerful strains of the "Song of the Vagabonds."

Stout Hearted Men

In the 1980s, the U.S. Marine Corps produced some very well thought out and polished advertisements on the theme "All we need are a few good men." The Corps was definitely correct in its manpower assessment. With a handful of superlative leaders, the mass of the people will follow toward the desired goal. So whether they are Marines, medieval knights like those indicated in one of the advertisements, or eighteenth century political fugitives from the French police like in the 1928 operetta *New Moon*, stouthearted men can accomplish wonders.

"Stout Hearted Men" was the most impressive number of *New Moon*, but three other songs by composer Sigmund Romberg (1887-1951) and lyricist Oscar Hammerstein II (1895-1960) are also worth noting. "Lover, Come Back to Me" is an excellent love ballad, and almost as good are the love duet "Wanting You" and the subtle and delicate "Softly as in a Morning Sunrise."

Romberg and Hammerstein seemingly had to develop these three more gentle and tender pieces to counteract the boisterous, powerful, and dominating mode of "Stout Hearted Men." Only one other well-known song from early twentieth century American stage productions approaches the dynamism of "Give me some men who are stout hearted men." The other rouser, "Song of the Vagabonds" from *The Vagabond King* (1925), probably influenced the composition of "Stout Hearted Men." But even emphatic "Vagabonds" could not match the strong musical and psychological impact of its later relative.

Strike Up the Band!

George Gershwin (1898-1937) and his collaborating lyricist brother Ira (1896-1983) wrote an abundance of standout songs. But few of them stood up and marched like the brilliant rouser "Strike Up the Band!" Introduced in the 1930 musical of the same title, "Strike Up" was the Gershwins' finest composition of the type and one of their overall best. It has been widely used for various occasions, including as a football fight song for the University of California at Los Angeles. (Ira adapted the tune for that purpose in 1936.)

Another well-known Gershwin piece in a march mode was the patriotic piece "Of Thee I Sing." The title song of the identically named 1931 Broadway show, "Of Thee" was one of the key numbers. The other top song from that production was "Love Is Sweeping the Country," a breezy, expansive tribute to romance.

The show won the Pulitzer Prize for drama, the first musical to be so honored. Much of the credit for the award has to go to the very skillful and imaginative lyrics by Ira. Perhaps nowhere is this more evident than in the novel combination of high reverence and close familiarity of the line "Of thee I sing, baby." (The "baby" referred to was the Statue of Liberty.)

Summertime

The warm, sunny, lazy days of summer have inspired a moderate amount of songs about that season. (It is too hot to work on a lot of them!) Around the turn of the century, lyricist Ren Shields and composer George Evans described the pleasures of life "In the Good Old Summertime" (1902). In recent years, "Those Lazy, Hazy, Crazy Days of Summer" (1963), words by Charles Tobias and music by Hans Carste, "Summertime, Summertime" (1958) by Sherm Feller and Tom Jameson, "The Summer Knows" or "The Theme from Summer of '42" (1971), words by Alan and Marilyn Bergman, music by Michel LeGrande, and "A Summer Place" (1960), a smooth instrumental by Max Steiner, also romanticized the mid-year doldrums.

The top dog of the dog days, however, is the steamy, simmering masterpiece "Summertime." The most impressive number of the great 1935 folk opera *Porgy and Bess,* "Summertime" is as vivid a reproduction of the season as music can create. That song, and the other highlights of the production "I Got Plenty o' Nuttin'" and "It Ain't Necessarily So," were written by composer George Gershwin (1898-1937) and lyricists Ira Gershwin (1896-1983) and Du Bose Heyward (1885-1940).

One of the most sensitive and subtle aspects of "Summertime" is that it requires a minimum amount of effort to sing or play it. It presents quite a contradiction–lazy requirements for performance coupled with an emotionally torrid and esthetically deep substance. In other words, like summer itself, it is both light and heavy.

Tea for Two

Because of its frequent usage as a dance number, "Tea for Two" could also be dubbed "Tea for Two Toes." It is a favorite of soft-shoe and tap dancers and even was recorded in a speeded up cha-cha version in 1958.

Whether it is danced to, sung, or played instrumentally, "Tea" is one of the all time popular classics. The most famous work of composer Vincent Youmans (1898-1946) and wordsmith Irving Caesar (1895-), it was written in 1924 for the 1925 hit musical *No, No Nanette.* (Caesar's lyrics were hastily provided late one night with the intent of starting all over the next day, but the inspired improvisation turned out to be an ideal fit.) Another song which helped build that show's success was "I Want to be Happy." A third Youmans-Caesar winner, from the later musical *Hit the Deck,* was "Sometimes I'm Happy" (1927).

Youmans also wrote the time-proven ballad "Time on My Hands" (1930) with lyricists Harold Adamson and Mack Gordon. Caesar also wrote "Is It True What They Say About Dixie?" (1936) with composer Gerald Marks and co-lyricist Sammy Lerner and "Swanee" (1919) with composer George Gershwin. But none of these could match "Tea for Two," which for Youmans and Caesar turned out to be "tea-riffic for two."

You Made Me Love You

There are political protest songs, social protest songs, and songs dealing with various other forms of confrontation. "You Made Me Love You" is also a protest song, but one associated with male-female relationships. Joe McCarthy's lyrics proclaim that "I didn't want to do it," but nevertheless the love affair so strongly resisted did come to pass.

McCarthy's coy lines and James V. Monaco's accompanying pensive melody were introduced by Al Jolson in the 1913 extravaganza *The Honeymoon Express*. Fanny Brice and Judy Garland also propelled their careers with this well-crafted musical complaint.

"You Made Me" was the only hit by McCarthy (1885-1943) and Monaco (1885-1945) as a team. Monaco also collaborated with lyricist William Jerome on "Row, Row, Row" (1912), not to be confused with the better-known anonymous 1881 American favorite "Row, Row, Row Your Boat." McCarthy also wrote "They Go Wild, Simply Wild Over Me" (1917) with composer Fred Fisher, "In My Sweet Little Alice Blue Gown" (1919) with composer Harry Tierney, and "I'm Always Chasing Rainbows" (1918) with composer Harry Carroll (melody based on Frederic Chopin).

Another well-known awkward or ambivalent love song is "I May Be Wrong But I Think You're Wonderful" (1929), words by Harry Ruskin and music by Henry Sullivan. Considering the often volatile patterns of romance, it's surprising that we aren't swamped by such pieces.

BROADWAY
1940 AND AFTER

Almost Like Being in Love

History books do not record the disappearance of a Scottish village in 1747. Yet, according to author/lyricist Alan Jay Lerner, the small community of Brigadoon, Scotland vanished in that year as part of a magic spell to ward off the evils of outside influences. Every 100 years the village comes to life once again for just 24 hours. Conveniently for Lerner and his composer collaborator Frederick Loewe, Brigadoon returned from the mists of the highlands just in time to provide them with their first hit musical in 1947.

A colorful, sensitive tale of romance, *Brigadoon* gave audiences a very charming production and one enduring ballad, "Almost Like Being in Love." Four years later Lerner (1918-1986) and Loewe (1904-1988) followed up with a less successful but good western locale show *Paint Your Wagon* (1951), which has left behind two reflective pieces, "I Talk to the Trees" and "They Call the Wind Maria." (In typical unconventional Lerner fashion "Maria" was pronounced as if it rhymed with "pariah.")

In 1956 Lerner and Loewe produced their unparalleled hit musical, *My Fair Lady.* That show, based on Bernard Shaw's masterpiece *Pygmalion*, introduced "I Could Have Danced All Night," "I've Grown Accustomed to Her Face," "On the Street Where You Live," and a fair amount of other well-known songs. Two years later two more notable L & L compositions, "Gigi" and "Thank Heaven for Little Girls," highlighted the Oscar-winning movie *Gigi.* Their last musical, *Camelot* (1960), was a moderately successful production that gave us "Camelot," "If Ever I Would Leave You," "Simple Joys of Maidenhood," and "What Do Simple Folk Do?" The show was a favorite of President John F. Kennedy, and his short tenure in office was, after his death, dubbed *Camelot.*

The careers of Lerner and Loewe were exhilarating and exciting. They created the mythical Brigadoon, re-created the legendary Camelot, and adapted a comedy classic into a huge musical classic of the Broadway stage. It must have been almost like being in love.

Another Op'nin', Another Show

Cole Porter's greatest musical, *Kiss Me Kate* (1948), owed a lot to William Shakespeare and possibly a little to Irving Berlin. The plot of the show was based on *The Taming of the Shrew*, and one of the top songs may well have been inspired by a number from Berlin's 1946 hit show *Annie Get Your Gun*.

Porter's opening rouser was "Another Op'nin', Another Show," which in style and purpose was quite similar to Berlin's spectacular "Show Business" or "There's No Business Like Show Business," written only two years before. If "Another Op'nin'" was an imitation it was an excellent one, as was the production as a whole. With both words and music by Porter (1891-1964), *Kiss Me Kate* presented some good standards as well as some cute lesser-known numbers. Comedy was provided by the request to "Brush Up Your Shakespeare," by the fickle "Always True to You in My Fashion," and by "Wunderbar," a parody of the Viennese waltz. Romance was inserted with the fine ballads "So In Love" and "Why Can't You Behave?"

But the best number was perhaps "Another Op'nin'," which both set the scene for the show about show people and established the high musical standards for the entire production. Not coincidentally, *Annie Get Your Gun* was also about two stubborn lovers working together in a traveling troupe. Annie's weapon happened to be a gun, Kate's an equally potent sharp tongue, but the similarities between the two musicals are not hard to discover.

Aquarius

Seldom does a musical list its most significant costuming in its title. But the 1968 show *Hair* does exactly that. Notorious for its onstage nudity, *Hair* was yet another sensation and scandal in one of the periods described by the old Chinese curse "May you live in interesting times."

But the absence of clothing in one sequence is not the real highlight of the production. Long after the shock of stark nakedness live in public had worn down, one of the songs from the show continued to live on. *Aquarius*, an inherently very good composition that became best known as one of the leading cultural symbols of its generation, still leads us toward "the dawning of the age of Aquarius" a generation later.

The best work of lyricists Gerome Ragni and James Rado and composer Galt MacDermot (1928-), "Aquarius" received a Grammy for the 1969 recording by the Fifth Dimension. Like another piece popularized by that group, "Up Up and Away" (Jim Webb, 1967), "Aquarius" was upbeat, imaginative, ethereal, and conducive to making us feel good. Such songs help to facilitate our survival in "interesting times," such as our present era.

Bewitched, Bothered, and Bewildered

This author is a bit bewitched, bothered, and bewildered at this point. Let us review for a moment what led up to the dilemma or, as the king in *The King and I* (1951) colorfully described it, the "puzzlement."

From 1920 to 1959, RH teams were producing musicals on Broadway. Starting in 1943, RH meant Rodgers and Hammerstein, or their Royal Highnesses, since that pair were the most successful Broadway figures of all time. Up to 1943, RH meant Rodgers and Hart, or regularly heard, another highly successful duo who created 27 shows in less than a quarter century.

The best-known musical by Richard Rodgers (1902-1979) and Lorenz Hart (1895-1943) was probably *Pal Joey* (1940). Yet that show only contained one really outstanding number, the lusty "Bewitched, Bothered and Bewildered." In contrast, three years earlier, another outstanding RH musical, *Babes in Arms* (1937), contained several well-known songs. The earlier show presented "My Funny Valentine," "The Lady Is a Tramp," "I Wish I Were in Love Again," "Where or When?", and "Johnny One Note."

But *Joey One Song* or *Pal Joey* is a lot more famous despite a lesser score. *Pal Joey*'s plot was apparently more appealing to audiences, and "Bewitched" is a most captivating, rich-toned love song, a real classic of popular music. Overall, though, the dominance of *Pal Joey* over *Babes in Arms* is somewhat hard to explain.

Cabaret

When Judy Garland made her biggest impact in motion pictures, it was as an idealistic and innocent teenager in *The Wizard of Oz* (1939). When Judy Garland's daughter, Liza Minnelli, made her biggest impact in a movie, it was as a cynical and less-than-innocent young woman in *Cabaret* (1972). The great societal changes in the generation or so between the pre-World War II period and the Vietnam era are mirrored in this most interesting contrast of artistic scenarios.

The Liza Minnelli film was a by-product of the 1966 Broadway musical about night life, naughtiness, nastiness, and Nazis in 1930s Germany. The show *Cabaret* was the most famous creation of composer John Kander (1927-) and lyricist W. Fred Ebb, and the beckoning title song "Cabaret" was their greatest long-term legacy. (Kander also wrote the music for another top show, *Zorba* in 1968.)

With enticing lines and a seductive tune, "Cabaret" reflects the pleasures and potential pitfalls of night club life in a big city. The song is still a frequently played standard, partly because of its inherent artistry and partly because it so well symbolizes the eternal beauty versus bizarreness contradictions of club atmosphere.

Diamonds Are a Girl's Best Friend

According to an old saying, dogs are a boy's or man's best friend. So what is the best friend of a girl or woman? If you believe the 1949 Broadway musical *Gentlemen Prefer Blondes*, the extremely hard chunks of crystallized carbon, which we call diamonds, are a girl's best friend. Since relationships are seldom forever, and diamonds always are, the delightful comic number expands on the long-range virtues of high carat jewelry.

But there is another school of thought about the behavior of gentlemen. A 1955 movie musical claimed that although they may give hard pretty stones to soft pretty blondes, *Gentlemen Marry Brunettes* at the end of the story. In the midst of this musical war about male-female attitudes, what gentlemen may feel about redheads seems to have been lost backstage.

The artistic gem from the minds of lyricist Leo Robin (1900-) and composer Jule Styne (1905-) will surely not endure as long as the geological gems described in their famous song, but "Diamonds Are a Girl's Best Friend" should be around for quite a while. It's a skillful as well as a unique piece, and touches upon a perennial dilemma. The pseudocynical theme of the words varies markedly from earlier idealistic lyrics by Robin, for example, "Beyond the Blue Horizon" (1930, composers Richard A. Whiting and W. Franke Harling), "Love in Bloom" (1934, composer Ralph Rainger), and "Love Is Just Around the Corner" (1934, composer Lewis E. Gensler). Perhaps after making so much money and gaining a fair amount of attention from these other hits, Robin by the late 1940s had come to the conclusion that fame and wealth are a man's best friend.

Ease on Down the Road

One of the various measures of success for a Broadway musical, motion picture, or radio or television program is how many sequels, imitators, or parodies it spawns. Yet some of the most important and popular productions in American cultural history have not been followed up by a lot of artistic offsprings.

For example, if you exclude movie versions of Broadway shows, there really have not been any effective sequels to *Gone with the Wind, Miracle on 34th Street, Oklahoma, My Fair Lady, Vertigo, The Sound of Music*, and similar classics. This absence of imitation is largely due to the feelings of richness, completeness, and satisfaction that these productions leave with audiences. It is very hard to follow a superlative act.

Not until 36 years after the appearance of the 1939 film masterpiece *The Wizard of Oz* and its great centerpiece "Over the Rainbow" did a significant afterthought dare to come into public view. About a generation and a half passed before the hit musical *The Wiz* (1975), a black variant on the adventures of Dorothy, ventured on the Great White Way of Broadway. With good songs by Charley Smalls, particularly the showstopper "Ease on Down the Road," *The Wiz* was one of the smashes of the 1970s, generating many greenbacks for all involved. (The road in the number, of course, was the yellow brick road leading to Oz.) Unfortunately, the 1978 movie sequel of the same name did not do very well at the box office and actually ended up in the red.

Hello, Dolly!

In arithmetic, four does not equal one. But on the Broadway stage, four successful musicals could end up generating only one outstanding, enduring song. Jerry Herman (1933-) was the composer and lyricist for a quartet of successful shows, *Milk and Honey* (1961), *Hello, Dolly!* (1964), *Mame* (1966), and *La cage aux folles* (1983).

From all these productions, however, only the title number "Hello, Dolly!" emerged as a big winner. "Dolly" the song was quite a phenomenon. Almost by itself it made the show a long-running hit. It greatly boosted the careers of Carol Channing, who played the lead role, and Louis Armstrong, who with his unique style delighted millions via an extraordinary recording. In an altered version, "Hello, Lyndon," it was used to launch the 1964 Presidential campaign of Lyndon Johnson. And, on top of it all, "Dolly" gained two Grammys.

Ironically, Herman's most notable composition, "Hello, Dolly!" may not have been entirely original. Herman was successfully sued by Mack David, composer of the 1948 song "Sunflower," for copyright infringement. "Dolly," who otherwise had such a charmed existence, finally lost one.

Hey, There

In the middle of the 1950s, it seemed as if another great Broadway musical team, in the Rodgers and Hammerstein or Lerner and Loewe tradition, had been born. Richard Adler and Jerry Ross scored big with critics and audiences with *Pajama Game* (1954) and *Damn Yankees* (1955).

But soon after the creation of *Damn Yankees*, Ross (1926-1955) died of a chronic respiratory disease, thus leaving Adler (1921-) without his very talented collaborator. Although Adler and Ross were both lyricists and composers, they had been unsuccessful as unpaired artists. With Ross gone, Adler's career reverted to the obscurity he suffered before the two joined together for their first hit "Rags to Riches" (1953).

That song became number one on the Hit Parade, and followed by a few other good pieces and the considerable success of *Pajama Game* and *Damn Yankees*, the fortunes of Adler and Ross figuratively changed from rags to riches. (Isn't it nice to compose a song that predicts your own future?) Several songs from the two shows remain as standards. "Heart" and "Whatever Lola Wants" from *Yankees* plus "Hernando's Hideaway" and "Hey, There" from *Game* have developed into perennials or classics. The taunting strains of "Lola," the encouraging sentiments of "Heart," the lively Latin dance rhythms and sense of mystery of "Hernando's," and "Hey, There," the sobering conversation of a lover with himself, collectively comprise a fine residue left by the brief Adler/Ross meteorite.

How Are Things in Glocca Morra?

Various types of "lanes" have been associated with American popular music. There is the constant "lovers' lane" that is affected by songs of romance. There was vocalist Frankie Laine, one of the top recording artists of the 1940s and 1950s. And there is composer Burton Lane (1912-) one of the better-known musicians of mid-century.

Finian's Rainbow, a hit 1947 musical by Lane and lyricist Edgar Yipsel Harburg (1898-1981), was Lane's biggest contribution. From that show came four good songs, "Look to the Rainbow," "Old Devil Moon," "When I'm Not Near the Girl I Love," and the main number, "How Are Things in Glocca Morra?"

Of course, since Glocca Morra is an imaginary place, we can never satisfactorily respond to the inquiry of that lovely Irish-style ballad. But we could answer a question such as "What else did Burton Lane do?" Among the other songs by Lane, with words by Ralph Freed, was an earlier musical question, "How About You?" (1941), which included a tribute to the recently departed George Gershwin. Innovation continued with "Feudin' and Fightin'" (1944), a comedy bit done with lyricist Al Dubin. This novelty's appearances included insertion in an animated cartoon about feuding hillbillies. Creativity again shone in another Lane standout, "I Hear Music" (1940), a cute love standard with words by Frank Loesser. The last important song by Lane was "On a Clear Day" (1965), a dreamy ballad with words by Alan Jay Lerner.

Burton was not hurtin' when it came to talent.

I Could Have Danced All Night

When Alan Jay Lerner (1918-1986) and Frederick Loewe (1904-1988) heard the critics' reviews and counted the money coming in, they could have danced all night. One of the longest-running musicals of all time, their *My Fair Lady* (1956) was perhaps the best such show to ever appear on the New York stage.

Lerner very skillfully adapted Bernard Shaw's play about a poor London flower girl who was transformed into a lady of breeding. He also developed clever lyrics to go with Loewe's well-crafted tunes and the result was a flower basket full of musical blossoms. There was the comedy rouser "Get Me to the Church on Time," which for years got the composers to the bank on time. There was "I've Grown Accustomed to Her Face," the grudging love ballad that kept the composers accustomed to fame and fortune. Then there was the linguistic novelty "The Rain in Spain," which kept the rain away from Lerner and Loewe's parade.

The fine romantic declaration "On the Street Where You Live" helped the show to live on the street named Broadway year after year. Talent, not luck, was involved with the humorous piece "With a Little Bit of Luck." And the wishing theme of "Wouldn't It Be Loverly?" was fulfilled by the show's great success.

Most of all there was "I Could Have Danced All Night," the reaction of the heroine, Eliza Doolittle, to her newfound status as a "duchess." That song and "On the Street" were possibly the best songs of the musical, but all of the seven compositions could individually be described as a little bit of a legend. Collectively they and the rest of the score, coupled with an exceptional plot, add up to a most loverly masterpiece of the American theater.

I Love Paris

A pseudonymous 1960 recording of "I Love Paris" was sufficient justification to dislike the fabled city. Grating, off-key, and performed in a contrived contralto, the parody version was rendered by songstress Jo Stafford. But Stafford did not just do comedy renditions. She also recorded in a straight and serious manner several top pop pieces.

In 1948 she did "Temptation" (1933), words by Arthur Freed and music by Nacio Herb Brown. In 1951 she popularized "Shrimp Boats" by Paul Mason Howard and Paul Weston. In 1952, her rendition of "Jambalaya" by Hank Williams was a top seller. A year later she recorded "Make Love to Me" (1953), lyrics by Bill Norvas and Allan Copeland and melody by Leon Rappolo and five others, plus "Teach Me Tonight," lyrics by Sammy Cahn and music by Gene DePaul. In summary, Stafford could sing quite well.

And Cole Porter (1891-1964), the renowned creator of musicals, could compose quite well. In 1953 he wrote the words and music for the hit show *Can-Can*. "I Love Paris," performed in a sentimental and reverent mood, was the main number. Porter's slow, hymnlike tribute to Paris was his last great song in a career that spanned over three decades. One of the elements that made Porter extra special is that he, like Irving Berlin, always devised the lyrics to go with his melodies. He was not overall as good as Berlin, but Porter's skillful blend of fine tunes and clever lyrics definitely made him one of the elite.

If I Were a Rich Man

As both a Broadway musical (1964) and a Hollywood movie (1971), *Fiddler on the Roof* was one of the most poignant productions in American theatrical history. The charming story of the joys and tribulations of a poor Jewish family in Tsarist Russia, bolstered by some very good music and fine performances, collectively created an exceptional experience for audiences. Among the memorable songs composed by lyricist Sheldon Harnick (1924-) and composer Jerry Bock (1928) were "Fiddler on the Roof"; "Matchmaker, Matchmaker"; "Sunrise," "Sunset," and "If I Were a Rich Man." With a catchy melody and very clever lyrics about the lowly milkman directly asking God what harm it would be if his status would be changed from a hard-working peasant to a wealthy man, "If I Were" was one of the best feature numbers ever to appear on a mid-Manhattan stage.

Harnick and Bock had had a fair amount of practice before creating their 1964 masterpiece. In 1956 Bock and lyricists George Weiss and Larry Holofcener collaborated on the successful show *Mr. Wonderful* from which two standards, "Mr. Wonderful" (which became Sammy Davis Jr.'s theme) and "Too Close for Comfort" emerged. Three years later came another hit, *Fiorello!*, with Harnick this time supplying the words for Bock's melodies. By the time Harnick and Bock had again joined their talents in *Fiddler*, they could from sunrise to sunset praise the matchmaker who turned them both into rich men.

The Impossible Dream

Dreaming is often a recurring theme in music. From the 1930s through the 1960s, a long night full of memorable "dream" songs saw the light of day. In the 1930s "Did You Ever See a Dream Walking?" (1933), words by Mack David and music by Harry Revel, and "All I Do Is Dream of You" (1934), words by Arthur Freed and music by Nacio Herb Brown, began the dream sequence. "Dream" (1944) by Johnny Mercer and "A Dream Is a Wish Your Heart Makes" (1949) by Mack David, Al Hoffman, and Jerry Livingston from the Disney feature *Cinderella* kept the 1940s dreaming. "Dream, Dream, Dream" (1954) with words by Mitchell Parish and music by Jimmy McHugh, "Dream Along with Me" (1955) by Carl Sigman, and "All I Have to Do Is Dream" (1958) by Boudleaux Bryant continued the dream through the 1950s. (The second piece became Perry Como's theme song.)

In the 1960s, when Martin Luther King Jr. was having his very possible dream, lyricist Joe Darion (1917-) and composer Mitch Leigh (1928-) were creating "The Impossible Dream." That inspiring show stopper, the key number from the 1965 musical *Man of La Mancha*, has become a favorite of male vocalists ever since. The excellent show was based on an earlier concept–Cervantes' masterful tale of the knight Don Quixote on his noble quest.

Was it a total coincidence that Quixote's imaginary musical dream on the New York stage took place at about the same time as King's real social and political dream on the center stage of U.S. history?

It's a Big, Wide Wonderful World

In the 1959 musical *Gypsy*, huge-voiced Ethel Merman declared that it's a "Small World." At least that was the opinion of composer Jule Styne and lyricist Stephen Sondheim.

If you want a second opinion on the matter, you may wish to consult John Rox. In 1940 Rox happily proclaimed "It's a Big, Wide Wonderful World" and the world has responded ever since by frequently echoing those lusty, life-loving lines. Appropriately, "Big, Wide Wonderful World" with its expansive melody and clever lyrics, was introduced in a revue entitled *All in Fun*.

Twenty-four years later Rox's sentiments were repeated, but not as gloriously, in Sid Tepper and Roy C. Bennett's "It's a Wonderful World" (1964). Only four years after that the charming ballad "What a Wonderful World" (1968) appeared. George Douglas and George David Weiss concocted this latter statement of optimism and the incomparable Louis Armstrong warmly rendered it on record.

All of these "wonderful world" declarations are good for the spirit. Sad or blue songs complement our mood at times, but we can't dwell forever in dark blue tones. So upbeat, uplifting light sky blue (or bright red or bright yellow) music like "It's a Big, Wide Wonderful World" is definitely a good prescription for our health whether or not we're in love.

Jesus Christ, Superstar

Jesus of Nazareth has been the main focus of Christianity for almost two milleniums. But until the 1971 rock musical *Jesus Christ, Superstar* appeared on Broadway, nobody had described Christ's enormous historical role as that of a "superstar." Of course, the concept of superstars really did not take hold until the "superhype" tendencies of recent decades, and therefore such a label probably would not have been readily affixed until the iconoclastic period of the 1960s and 1970s. Although rendering to Christ this most audacious term may seem to some to be sacrilegious, it can truly be said that no one else was ever more deserving.

The superstar of the show was the splendid musical proclamation "Jesus Christ, Superstar." It doesn't compare with "The Messiah," which also is emphatic and has the same basic theme, but "Superstar" is about as good as a religiously oriented composition can get in a pop rock context.

The creators of the 1971 production, 23-year-old Andrew Lloyd Webber (1948-) and Tim Rice, also collaborated on another hit, *Evita* in 1978. After that Lloyd Webber, without Rice, scored with the productions *Cats* (1982) and *Phantom of the Opera* (1987). Lloyd Webber's musicals are surely not at the level of the great productions of Rodgers and Hammerstein of a generation earlier, but at least for the 1970s and 1980s, Lloyd Webber is Broadway's best candidate for "superstar."

June Is Bustin' Out All Over

The big dance sequence of the musical *Carousel* (1945), "June Is Bustin' Out All Over," has gone beyond the status of a standard. With parodies and humor such as the joke about the overly fat woman, "June is Bustin'" has attained the level of a legend or stereotype. Part of its fame is due to the emphatic and enthusiastic melody by Richard Rodgers (1902-1979). Another part of its fame is due to the very imaginative and well-manipulated lyrics by Oscar Hammerstein II (1895-1960).

Much of the song's success, however, is due to the concept of celebrating the greatly anticipated arrival of full-blown spring, especially when you live in the northern climate of Maine. The unbridled joy of finally having warm, sunny weather is the prime motivator for the number.

"June Is Bustin'" is the only real rouser in the show, though. There are several other fine or even classic compositions, but they tend to be more subdued or poignant. The lilting "Carousel Waltz," which leads us into the tragic tale, the excellent love duet "If I Loved You," and the pensive ballad "What's the Use of Wond'rin'?" all suggest bittersweet themes. Even Bill's "Soliloquy," an extended solo, is alternatively expansive and reserved in mood. And the outstanding spiritual finale, "You'll Never Walk Alone," is a blend of sadness and hope.

Carousel was not the very best show by Rodgers and Hammerstein. But with its story of love, death, and faith in life, plus a splendid score, it is for many a sentimental favorite.

Luck Be a Lady

In the outstanding 1950 musical *Guys and Dolls*, the main male character, a gambler and high-liver, musically pleads, "Luck be a lady tonight." Well, luck was not only a one night lady for Frank Loesser, the composer and lyricist of the show, but was for about a quarter of a century a most gracious grand dame for his artistic fortunes.

After classic individual songs like "Heart and Soul" (1938), words by Loesser and music by Hoagy Carmichael, and "Praise the Lord and Pass the Ammunition" (1942) by Loesser alone, he became one of the top creative persons on Broadway. It started in 1948 with *Where's Charley?*, followed by *Guys and Dolls*, *The Most Happy Fella* (1956), and *How to Succeed in Business Without Really Trying* (1961). In all of these hit musicals, Loesser (1910-1969) wrote both the clever lyrics and the good tunes.

Guys and Dolls was Loesser's most famous show. In the score along with the dramatic "Luck Be a Lady" were "A Bushel and a Peck," a charming comedy love piece, "If I Were a Bell," an upbeat exclamation of infatuation, and the moody "I've Never Been in Love Before." Another standard, "A Woman in Love" ("Your Eyes Are the Eyes of a Woman in Love") was added by Loesser to the 1955 movie veision.

So for quite a while, guys and dolls in Manhattan did not have to ask "Where's Frankie?" They all knew that he was a most happy fella who seemed to succeed on Broadway without really trying.

Mack the Knife

"Mack the Knife" was written by Marc the knife. Marc Blitzstein (1905-1964), a significant American composer and lyricist, was a cutting social radical who strongly incorporated his political views in his artistic works, including Broadway musicals. Ironically, Blitzstein's philosophical leanings are totally out of view to most listeners when his best-known achievement, the words for "Mack the Knife," are sung.

"Mack," also known as "Moritat," was the highlight of the 1954 off Broadway musical, *The Three Penny Opera*. "Moritat," which apparently comes from the German words "mord" (murder) and "tat" (deed), was an accurate description of the grisly tale unfolded by Blitzstein's morbid lyrics. But the title "Mack the Knife" had more appeal for audiences than the gruesome alternate, not that the skillful words and excellent melody needed much help.

"Moritat" actually goes back to 1928. It was the title of a song in the world-famous production, *Die Dreigroschenoper*, which premiered in Berlin. The music of the ballad and the whole opera were by German-American composer Kurt Weill (1900-1950), and the song lyrics and opera text were by the renowned German dramatist Bertolt Brecht (1898-1956). Blitzstein wrote new English words to accompany Weill's tune when the 1928 show was revived in New York in 1954, a few years after Weill's death. When Weill created the music, he was influenced by the "moritats" or musical stories performed at street fairs in Europe that relate the unsavory crimes committed by various fiends.

The original story about Mackie and his escapades goes back even further, to 1728. Another famous production, the enduring English phenomenon *The Beggar's Opera* by John Gay and John Christopher Pepusch, was the first link in this centuries-long theatrical chain that meandered from early eighteenth-century London to early twentieth-century Berlin to mid-twentieth-century New York.

And the chain doesn't end there. "Mack the Knife," in its final form, was recorded a number of times in the 1950s and became one of the top hits of that decade and a continuing favorite ever since. The most successful disk was Bobby Darin's 1959 version, which won a Grammy.

The strangest facet to this tale of historical twists and knife twists is that "Mack," with all its blood and sordidness, is often regarded as a composition conducive to romance.

My Way

Musically it may not be the very best song ever written, but psychologically it is one of the more appealing popular compositions of the twentieth century. For most of us, to be able to claim "I did it my way" is a badge of honor. A good ballad intrinsically, "My Way," with fine 1969 lyrics by Paul Anka to accompany a melody by Jacques Revaux, adds the special extra element of self-pride for the independent person.

People who lived through the turbulent 60s understand that there were a very large number of independent persons during that era who did it their way. As a mirror of that widespread outlook, there actually were two songs of the '60s with the title "My Way." The much more famous piece, lovingly adopted and popularized by Frank Sinatra, was the above-mentioned duo of Revaux and Anka.

The other and also successful "My Way" comes from a British musical with as iconoclastic and free-spirited a title as mainstream productions ever get. *The Roar of the Greasepaint–The Smell of the Crowd* (1965), with words and music by Anthony Newley (1931-) and Leslie Bricusse (1931-), was one of the more successful shows of its decade. Three years earlier, in 1962, Newley and Bricusse also scored with *Stop the World–I Want to Get Off* and "What Kind of Fool Am I?"–its standout closing number. In addition to creating good musicals, the two artists showed that they could come up with inventive show titles, dashes and all.

Although there is no way that Newley and Bricusse could be favorably compared to the great musical duos of Rodgers and Hammerstein or Lerner and Loewe, the Britishers did have the satisfaction of knowing that they personally lived up to their "My Way" song. They also, along with Anka and Sinatra, could be proud to have expressed musically one of the most dominant credos of our era.

New York, New York

There is a most interesting cultural progression that can be inferred from the prominent trio of songs about New York City. The first, "The Sidewalks of New York" by James W. Blake and Charles B. Lawlor, reflects the relative simplicity and innocence of the city in 1894. The second, "Manhattan," reflects the town's increased worldliness and sophistication by 1925 (a few years before the George Washington Bridge, Radio City Music Hall, and the Empire State Building were erected). And the third, "New York, New York" (1944) clearly shows the brashness and toughness that was overtaking the metropolis around the end of World War II.

Written by the outstanding composer Leonard Bernstein (1918-1990) with lyricists Betty Comden (1915-) and Adolph Green (1915-) for Bernstein's first Broadway musical *On the Town*, "New York, New York" was a reasonably accurate mirror of the ambivalence of New York at that time. A large amount of excitement and pride was combined with an overall small amount of softness and gentleness. Or, in other words, "New York, New York, it's a wonderful town" (if you know your way around and don't weaken). (The 1944 "New York, New York" should not be confused with the 1977 song "New York, New York" from the film of the same name, which was created by composer John Kander and W. Fred Ebb, and which includes the line, "If I can make it there, I'll make it anywhere.")

By the time of Bernstein's most famous musical, *West Side Story* (1957), the psychological depiction of New York had deteriorated to the savage, ugly, cynical slums. Again, though, it wasn't all one-sided. Love, beauty, and hope also found their way into the lives of the rival ghetto gangs. When the next significant song about the city comes to life, what will it suggest about life in America's biggest population center? Prognosticators and futurists, any predictions?

Oh, What a Beautiful Mornin'

The opening scene of the 1943 musical *Oklahoma!* featured the upbeat, graceful waltz "Oh, What a Beautiful Mornin'." As if Richard Rodgers (1902-1979) and Oscar Hammerstein II (1895-1960) could predict their future unmatched fortunes on the Broadway stage, that number, their first together, turned out to be the beautiful morning of a new era in American theatrical history. The tremendous success of *Oklahoma!* was followed by four other masterpieces, *Carousel* (1945), *South Pacific* (1949), *The King and I* (1951), and *The Sound of Music* (1959), plus several other good musicals.

The score of *Oklahoma* was, without exaggeration, superb. There is not one weak song in the entire show. Between the outstanding "Beautiful Morning" and the brilliant rousing finale "Oklahoma!" are several standards and semi-standards. Still very memorable are "The Farmer and the Cowman," a sparkling comedic rivalry number; "I Cain't Say No," the amusing complaint of a free-loving young woman; "Kansas City," another delightful, bouncy piece about life in the "up-to-date" city; "The Surrey with the Fringe on Top," a charming love classic; and three fine romantic ballads, "Many a New Day," "Out of My Dreams," and "People Will Say We're in Love."

Oklahoma! by any standard, must rank as one of the top five musicals ever. (Another would be *South Pacific.*) Like the corn in the lyrics of the rural yet sophisticated "Beautiful Mornin'" appetizer, the show climbed clear up to the sky. Like some other lines in the same piece, Rodgers and Hammerstein had everything going their way.

Send in the Clowns

If you are familiar with Mozart's famous 1787 classical delight "Eine Kleine Nachtmusik" ("A Little Night Music"), you know that it is a lively, uplifting piece. And if you were unfamiliar with the song "Send in the Clowns," you might well guess that it is a lively, comical composition. So with a song thus named being from a musical entitled *A Little Night Music*, it is far from ridiculous to presume a positive, upbeat mood for the song.

Yet "Clowns" is a very sad, even depressing ballad. The centerpiece of the successful 1973 musical, "Clowns" won a Grammy award and has become a standard since then. *A Little Night Music* was the work of composer and lyricist Stephen Sondheim (1930-). But as good as this show was, Sondheim was strongly involved with two even better Broadway productions, *Gypsy* (1959) and *West Side Story* (1957). Sondheim was the lyricist with Jule Styne for *Gypsy*, which featured the rousing standard "Everything Is Coming Up Roses," and with Leonard Bernstein for *West Side Story*, which showcased the classic ballads "Maria" and "Tonight." Although Sondheim has not reached the level of such greats as Rodgers and Hammerstein, Cole Porter, Lerner and Loewe, or even Frank Loesser, to be a major contributor to three top shows indicates that you have written more than a little night music.

Seventy-Six Trombones

The blaring of 76 trombones gets a lot of attention. And that is exactly what the 1957 musical *The Music Man* received. The show was one of the most famous and best received productions of the decade and made the fictitious River City, Iowa and the imaginary Marian the librarian into household words.

The Music Man also made its librettist, composer, and lyricist, Meredith Willson, into a celebrity. Willson's sentimental, old-fashioned, hometown plot and direct, unsubtle music charmed audiences everywhere. One of the more memorable songs was the tender love ballad "Till There Was You." But by far the main number was the resounding, brash, stimulating march "Seventy-Six Trombones," which instantly became a hit throughout the country and has remained a favorite since then. Incidentally, have you ever wondered why the number "76" was used? In addition to the alliterative values of "seventy" and "six," one suspects that the choice of that particular number was because of the very special historic and patriotic significance of 76 (1776).

So there was much commotion over *The Music Man* and its leading composition. Yet the rest of the career of Willson (1902-1984) was collectively not as successful as the one big parade of fame and fortune started by the 1957 show. Two subsequent Broadway productions, *The Unsinkable Molly Brown* (1960) and *Here's Love* (1963) were moderately well received, but did not have any songs of major impact except for the lively song of determination, "I Ain't Down Yet" from *Molly Brown*. Away from the musical theater, Willson created a pair of fairly well-known pieces,"May the Good Lord Bless and Keep You Till We Meet Again" (1950) and "It's Beginning to Look Like Christmas" (1951). Willson covered romance, patriotism, willpower, spirituality, and Christmas pleasures in his five top songs, and in doing so covered a lot of Americana.

Shall We Dance?

As many people know, Yul Brynner played the part of the King of Siam in the 1951 musical *The King and I* and in its 1956 movie adaptation. After all that was the role that made Brynner famous. But do you know the name of the king Brynner portrayed so magnificently? The answer to this trivia quiz is "Mongkut," a monarch who strongly guided the destiny of mid-nineteenth-century Thailand.

The story of Mongkut and the English governess Anna is one of the most charming in U.S. stage history. Although the score by Richard Rodgers (1902-1979) and Oscar Hammerstein II (1895-1960) is not as compelling as their other exceptional musicals, the overall impact of the production is comparable. The combination of good western-style music overlaid on attractive oriental motifs was in its time and is still today a most pleasant experience.

Among the numbers were Anna's cute approach to the king's numerous children, "Getting to Know You." There was also the nostalgic romantic ballad "Hello, Young Lovers" and the spirit-lifting "I Whistle a Happy Tune."

The main piece, perhaps, was "Shall We Dance?", a duet of admiration and respect between Anna and the king. This was not the usual song of physical love between a man and woman, but instead one demonstrating psychological appreciation. This atypical feature of the composition, plus its inherent excellent qualities, make "Shall We Dance?," like the rest of the show, a thing extraordinary.

Show Business

"Show Business," or "There's No Business Like Show Business," has become sort of an unofficial national anthem of American show business. Just as "You Oughta Be in Pictures" (1934, by lyricist Edward Heyman and musician Dana Suesse) represents the movies, "Show Business" is the perennial fanfare for the entire entertainment industry. At the very least it is the leading and most obvious musical symbol of the theater in the U.S. and to some extent elsewhere.

Yet, reportedly, it was originally just an afterthought in Irving Berlin's great 1946 musical, *Annie Get Your Gun.* After the score had been completed and preparation for the Broadway production had begun, there was a long interlude between scenes in which stage props and scenery needed to be moved. To cover this gap in the midst of the show, Berlin supplied the music of "Show Business." In time, the song became a full-fledged component of the musical and, ironically, its rousing centerpiece.

In the Broadway production, "Show Business" was exuberantly belted out by Ethel Merman and company. In the 1950 movie version of *Annie Get Your Gun* it was delightfully proclaimed by Betty Hutton and associates. And in the 1954 movie musical *There's No Business Like Show Business* it was rendered by none other than Marilyn Monroe. Other performances of "Show Business" in various contexts have been legion, including parodies such as "Shoe business" and "Snow business." It is quite understandable why this enthusiastic, bustling phenomenon was among Berlin's five personal favorites, along with his other classics "Easter Parade," "White Christmas," "Always," and "God Bless America."

God bless the memory of the pop genius Irving Berlin (1888-1989).

Some Enchanted Evening

The whole score of the great Rodgers and Hammerstein musical *South Pacific* (1949) was inspired. The mystical description of mysterious "Bali Ha'i," the lively comedy numbers "There is Nothin' Like a Dame," "A Cockeyed Optimist," "I'm in Love with a Wonderful Guy," and "I'm Gonna Wash That Man Right Outa My Hair," plus the tender love ballads "This Nearly Was Mine" and "Younger Than Springtime," collectively comprise one of the finest aggregate of standards in one show.

The real showstopper, in a production that has several, is the magnificent proclamation "Some Enchanted Evening." A strong, emotional, capturing number, and a perfect vehicle for a deep, resonant, projecting male voice, "Enchanted Evening" emits clear touches of magic as well as passion. Most love affairs do not start with such a "love at first sight" impact as portrayed in the lyrics, but wouldn't it be superb if such were the case?

One of the indirect points of the song is that most relationships begin slowly and tentatively. If instant attraction were the normal process, then first meetings would not be that special occasion or enchanted evening.

"Some Enchanted Evening" also applies to the whole show. At initial hearing the musical is pure delight. After many repetitions, *South Pacific* remains as beautiful, pleasant, and easy to take as the region in which it is set.

The Sound of Music

The beginning scene in the 1959 live Broadway production was quite compelling, but the extra flexibility of camera work in the 1965 movie version made the opening of *The Sound of Music* most exhilarating. With the majestic mountains of Austria as a stimulating introduction to the film, followed by a rapid focus down to the picture of the young nun standing alone on a verdant hill, nothing but an exceptional composition would have fit the situation.

The brilliant title song, "The Sound of Music," more than fulfilled the expectations of moviegoers as it did for stage audiences. "Sound" was the centerpiece of one of the most successful of all musicals and was supported by several other fine numbers as well as a winner of a story line. Inspiration abounded in "Climb Every Mountain." Fun with the Von Trapp children flowed with "My Favorite Things" and "Do, Re, Mi." The nuns' dilemma was expressed in "Maria." Teenage love fumbled around in "You Are Sixteen." And the love of beautiful flowers and of country became manifest in "Edelweiss."

"The Sound of Music" was not just the main song in the production, however. Since this was the last collaboration of the great musician Richard Rodgers (1902-1979) and the word master Oscar Hammerstein II (1895-1960), the composition was in effect a symbol of their contribution to the world's culture as well as their joint musical farewell. Since Rodgers and Hammerstein together and with other collaborators were the two most prominent figures of the American musical theater, it was most fitting that this parting piece was both beautiful and poignant.

Stranger in Paradise

There's a not so great joke about a gambler in Las Vegas singing "Hold my hand, I'm a stranger with a pair of dice." That parody, of course, referred to the excellent ballad "Stranger in Paradise," which was a big hit in the mid-1950s and has been a favorite in the following decades.

The authors of the song were also gamblers. Several times they gambled on adapting the music of famous serious composers as the foundation for Broadway musicals and twice the odds came in their favor. The first stage success for George "Chet" Forrest (1915-) and Robert Wright (1914-) was *Song of Norway* (1944), with lyrics by Forrest and Wright and music based on the works of the Norwegian classical composer Edvard Grieg. The top number was "Strange Music."

Their second winner was *Kismet* (1953), again with lyrics by Forrest and Wright, but this time the major Russian composer Alexander Borodin was the musical lender. Three songs have endured from that show, the mystical "Baubles, Bangles and Beads," the emotional love piece "And This Is My Beloved," and most of all the beautiful "Stranger in Paradise." The lyrics of the last song fit well with the sense of exoticism and expansiveness in the theme borrowed from Borodin's *Polovtsian Dances.* Forrest and Wright did not create new music, but they sometimes chose well and as a result made some fine additions to the popular repertory.

One other Forrest-Wright effort should be mentioned. In 1937, the piece "Donkey Serenade" was inserted into a screen version of the Rudolf Friml operetta *The Firefly.* In typical Forrest-Wright fashion, they wrote the lyrics and derived the melody from a 1923 Friml song. This time they didn't extract from classical music, but instead from a composer of classic operettas like *The Firefly, Rose Marie*, and *The Vagabond King*.

They Say It's Wonderful

Many Broadway musicals have only one key song that preserves the memory of the production. For example, the show *Fine and Dandy* (1930) is noted only for the title song, "Fine and Dandy," by Paul James (lyricist) and Kay Swift (composer). And the sole famous piece from *Cabin in the Sky* (1940) is the ballad "Taking a Chance on Love" by lyricists John Latouche and Ted Fetter with composer Vernon Duke.

So if Irving Berlin (1888-1989) had settled for one outstanding song, the classic "Show Business" (or "There's No Business Like Show Business") in his 1946 musical *Annie Get Your Gun*, the show would still probably be preserved. But with typical Berlin largess, he had to compose a half dozen other standard songs thus making *Annie Get Your Gun* one of the very best musicals in American stage history. These include the humorous competition song "Anything You Can Do" and its wiser counterpart "You Can't Get a Man With a Gun." Then, Annie Oakley's two bouncy country novelties, "Doin' What Comes Natur'lly" and "Sun in the Mornin'," must be mentioned. Also included were the splendid pair of love ballads, "The Girl That I Marry" and, the incomparable, "They Say It's Wonderful."

Few other compositions have better captured the ambivalent sentiments of romance than the lines "They say that falling in love is wonderful, is wonderful, so they say." However, there is nothing ambivalent about the qualities of this enduring song. It is one of the most sensitive, subtle, and at the same time sensuous tributes to love ever written. In the show, furthermore, it helped Annie not only get her gun but her man too.

Tonight

One of the best-known songs from the 1957 musical *West Side Story* was the bubbly bauble "I Feel Pretty." But there was nothing pretty about the locale or plot of the production. Set in the rough, tough, unattractive slums of the West Side of Manhattan, the show strongly portrayed the antagonisms of rival youth gangs. In the tradition of Romeo and Juliet, Maria, a young Puerto Rican woman involved with one of the gangs, and Tony, a member of the despised enemy group, fall in love in spite of the atmosphere of racial and overall hatred. Tony and one of the Puerto Rican gang members, Bernardo, are murdered, bloodily punctuating the already grim tale. But all is not negative, for definite touches of love and beauty are interspersed into the scenario.

Both the love and the beauty are brought out in the two memorable love songs, "Maria" and "Tonight." The latter song, the musical signature of the show, clearly reflects the classical music training of prestigious Leonard Bernstein (1918-1990). *West Side Story* was the last in a series of four good Broadway enterprises by the multitalented composer, conductor, and media personality. *On the Town* (1944) features the breezy number "New York, New York" and the upbeat standard "Lucky to Be Me." *Wonderful Town* (1953) produced the tongue-in-cheek curiosity "Ohio." (The lyrics for the 1944 and 1953 shows were by Betty Comden and Adolph Green who also collaborated with composer Jule Styne on "Just in Time" (1956), "Make Someone Happy" (1960), and "The Party's Over" (1956).) *Candide* (1956) was highlighted by the brilliant overture.

West Side Story, however, was Bernstein's stage masterpiece. His fine score, accompanied by very capable lyrics by Stephen Sondheim, contributed greatly in making the show one of the best musicals in a decade of exceptional musicals. One of the other fine Broadway treats of the 1950s, incidentally, was *Gypsy* (1959) on which Sondheim (1930-) collaborated with Jule Styne. That production, the colorful story of Gypsy Rose Lee with the memorable rouser "Everything Is Coming Up Roses," is an interesting contrast with *West Side Story* with its dark hues and relatively subdued score.

Try to Remember

When wordsmith Tom Jones (1928-) and composer Harvey Schmidt (1929) created their charming and famous off-Broadway musical *The Fantasticks*, they probably never envisioned the show's fantastically long run. As of the writing of this book, the 1960 production was still going strong and appeared to be protected by some magic spell of eternal life.

On the negative side, the huge perpetual artistic shadow cast by the show's main prop, the wall between the families, seems to have relegated any other creativity by Jones and Schmidt to relative obscurity. (For those not familiar with the plot, the wall is built by two close friends who hope that by strictly prohibiting a romantic relationship between their children they thereby will encourage a surreptitious love affair. Their unconventional reverse psychology ploy works as if devised by the devil himself.)

The music from the show is nowhere as fantastic as the production's longevity, but one number remains a bit of a classic. "Try to Remember," a slow nostalgic ballad, has managed to more or less gain the status of a standard. Curiously, this key song is such a prediction of the show's tendency toward infinity that one senses that something spooky has been conjured up. If the show mystically drifts through many more years, the denizens of the New York theater world may start to comment, "Try to remember when the original run of *The Fantasticks* was not haunting our city."

What I Did for Love

Did anyone keep the statistics on how many pairs of shoes the dancers from *A Chorus Line* wore out during its fantastic 15-year run on Broadway? If you had the exclusive contract for supplying footwear for the 1975-1990 show, you would have been as welcome at the New York banks as were composer Marvin Hamlisch and lyricist Edward Kleban. Although the production had its share of good music, the strongest features of the celebrated musical were a good story line and superlative dancing.

The leading song from *A Chorus Line* was "What I Did for Love," an effective romantic ballad. Whether or not "What I Did" becomes a perennial classic remains to be seen. Quite possibly it may be swallowed up in time by the overwhelming historical aura of the show's endurance. While many songs from Broadway are far better known than the musicals that spawned them, the opposite may be the case for "What I Did" and *A Chorus Line.*

Hamlisch also wrote another song of some note, "They're Playing My Song" from the 1979 musical of the same name. With good words by Carole Bayer Sager and a catchy melody, "They're Playing" might well be more durable than "What I Did." Ironically, the key song from the shorter running production may survive longer in public favor than the key song from the longer running show.

MOVIES

All the Way

The 1957 motion picture *The Joker Is Wild* was the film biography of comedian Joe E. Lewis. "All the Way," which was introduced by Frank Sinatra in that production, was created to emphasize the loss of voice by Lewis. After the opening limited-range bars, the notes for the words "all the way" leap way up high, beyond the vocal capability of Lewis, thus setting up a scene of pathos.

"All the Way" had a much different effect on Sinatra, whose fine rendition of the song helped keep him all the way at the top, and on its composers, who took the receipts from the song all the way to the bank. But Sammy Cahn (1913-1992), who wrote the words, and James Van Heusen (1913-1990), who wrote the music, were well accustomed to visiting their local financial institutions.

During the 1950s and early 1960s they also kept Sinatra going to the recording studio with a series of standards. In addition to "All the Way" the popular "Love and Marriage" (1955), "The Tender Trap" (1955), "Come Fly With Me" (1958), "High Hopes" (1959), "The Second Time Around" (1961), and "My Kind of Town" (1964) are also noteworthy. "All," "High," and "Love" all won high, lovely awards. On top of gathering legal tender, Sammy and Jimmy, along with Frankie, their kind of singer, flew together in the stratosphere of musical honors three times around.

Around the World

The word "young" springs up from time to time in popular music. There are several well-known ballads with "young" in the title, for example, "Younger than Springtime" (1949) and "Hello, Young Lovers" (1951) by lyricist Oscar Hammerstein II and composer Richard Rodgers, "Too Young" (1951) by lyricist Sylvia Dee and composer Sid Lippman, "Young and Foolish" (1954) by lyricist Arnold B. Morwitt and composer Albert Hague, and "Young at Heart" (1954) by lyricist Carolyn Leigh and composer Johnny Richards.

There also have been several songwriters with the surname "Young." In the first half of the century two lyricists, Joe Young (1898-1946) and Rida Johnson Young (1869-1926), were affiliated with some memorable compositions. Joe Young, not to be confused with the mighty ape of the same name, wrote "I'm Gonna Sit Right Down and Write Myself a Letter" (1935) with composer Fred E. Ahlert, "Dinah" (1924) with co-lyricist Sam M. Lewis and composer Harry Akst, "My Mammy" (1921) and "How Ya Gonna Keep 'em Down on the Farm?" (1919) with co-lyricist Sam M. Lewis and composer Walter Donaldson, "Five Foot Two, Eyes of Blue" (1925) and "I'm Sitting on Top of the World" (1925) with co-lyricist Sam M. Lewis and composer Ray Henderson, "Rockabye Your Baby with a Dixie Melody" (1918) with co-lyricist Sam M. Lewis and composer Jean Schwartz, "Starlight" (1931) with composer Bernice Petkere, and "In a Shanty in Old Shanty Town" (1933) with words and music by Young, John Siras, and Little Jack Little.

Rida Johnson Young wrote "Ah, Sweet Mystery of Life" (1910), "Tramp, Tramp, Tramp Along the Highway" (1910), and "I'm Falling in Love with Someone" (1910) with Victor Herbert, and "Will You Remember?" or "Sweetheart, Sweetheart, Sweetheart" (1917) with Sigmund Romberg.

A third songwriter named "Young" was composer Victor Young (1900-1956). Among his works are "When I Fall in Love" (1952) with lyricist Edward Heyman, "My Foolish Heart" (1949) with lyricist Ned Washington, "Golden Earrings" (1946) with lyricists Jay Livingston and Ray Evans, "Sweet Sue" (1928) with lyricist Will J. Harris, and "Around the World" (1956) with lyricist Harold Adamson (1906-). The last song, but without the lyrics ever being used, was the theme for the spectacular motion picture *Around the World in Eighty Days.* (Four other collaborations by Adamson, incidentally, were "Comin' in on a Wing and a Prayer" [1943] and "It's a Most Unusual Day" [1948] with composer Jimmy McHugh, plus "Time on My Hands" [1930] with co-lyricist Mack Gordon and composer Vincent Youmans and the theme for the *I Love Lucy* television series [1951] with Eliot Daniel.)

This essay has cursorily carried us around parts of the world of popular music just as the expansive 1956 film fleetingly circled the globe with a wide screen full color camera. With an open mind, there certainly is more than one way to travel in style.

Beyond the Blue Horizon

No matter how well Richard A. Whiting played in Peoria, his hometown, his music did well elsewhere. Among the early compositions by Whiting (1891-1938) were "Some Sunday Morning" (1917), words by Gus Kahn and Raymond B. Egan and music by Whiting, "Till We Meet Again" (1918), words by Egan and music by Whiting, "Ain't We Got Fun" (1921), words and music by Whiting, "Sleepy Time Gal" (1925), words by Joseph R. Alden and Egan and music by Ange Lorenzo and Whiting, and "She's Funny That Way" (1928), words by Whiting and music by Neil Moret.

Later Whiting songs included "Beyond the Blue Horizon" (1930), words by Leo Robin (1900-) and music by Whiting and W. Franke Harling, "You're an Old Smoothie" (1932), words by Bud De Sylva and music by Whiting and Nacio Herb Brown, "On the Good Ship Lollipop" (1934), words by Sidney Clare and music by Whiting, "Too Marvelous for Words" (1937), words by Johnny Mercer and music by Whiting, and "Hooray for Hollywood" (1938), words by Mercer and music by Whiting.

Perhaps the most interesting of Whiting's songs were "Lollipop," which was sung by little Shirley Temple in the 1934 movie *Bright Eyes* and by big "Tiny Tim" on television in the late 1960s, and "Blue Horizon." The latter piece made quite an impact at its introduction in the film *Monte Carlo*. With the camera showing Jeanette MacDonald sitting in a moving train singing the song, accompanied by harmonizing peasants in the fields outside, the orchestration on the soundtrack simulated the rhythms and sounds of the train. To us today this appears to be nothing special, but at the time the effect was sensational.

Blues in the Night

In American popular music, the word "blue" has two widely contrasting meanings. Blue can sometimes represent a bright, attractive color. For example, there are "Blue Skies" (1927) by Irving Berlin, "My Blue Heaven" (1927) with words by George Whiting and music by Walter Donaldson, "Where the Blue of the Night Meets the Gold of the Day" (1931), with words my Roy Turk and Bing Crosby and music by Fred E. Ahlert, "Blue Hawaii" (1937) with words by Leo Robin and music by Ralph Rainger, and "Blue Suede Shoes" (1956) by Carl Lee Perkins.

More often, though, blue represents a despondent or melancholy mood. There is even a type of black jazz called the blues because of the presence of so-called "blue notes." On top of having blue notes such compositions are in addition typically sad or psychologically blue. The classic blues song is W. C. Handy's 1914 "Saint Louis Blues." Other well-known relatives are "The Wang, Wang Blues" (1921), with words by Gus Mueller and Buster Johnson and music by Henry Busse; "The Birth of the Blues" (1926), with words by Bud De Sylva and Lew Brown and music by Ray Henderson; "Blue Again" (1930), with words by Dorothy Fields and music by Jimmy McHugh; "Blue Moon" (1934), with words by Lorenz Hart and music by Richard Rodgers; "Blues in the Night" (1941), with words by Johnny Mercer and music by Harold Arlen, and "Blue Tango" (1952), an instrumental by Leroy Anderson.

The song by Mercer (1909-1976) and Arlen (1905-1986) is one of the top blues pieces. Originally it was created for a 1941 motion picture tentatively to be named *Hot Nocturne*. However, the initial reaction to the composition was so positive that the film title was changed to *Blues in the Night*. According to the great Jerome Kern, Mercer and Arlen's "Blues" should have won the Academy Award that year instead of Kern's "The Last Time I Saw Paris" because the latter was not specifically written for the cinema. But, as is indicated in various places in this volume, Mercer and Arlen gained plenty of other recognition, including Oscars for other years.

Days of Wine and Roses

If you haven't seen the 1962 motion picture, *Days of Wine and Roses*, the plot involved the tragedy of a chronically alcoholic couple. Therefore, the film was more about wine than about roses.

For the composers of the theme song, however, everything came up roses with their beautiful, moody ballad. Written by lyricist Johnny Mercer (1909-1976) and musician Henry Mancini (1924-), "Days of Wine and Roses" won an Oscar and two Grammys. Another work by this duo, "Moon River" (1961), similarly earned the same three awards and was a tremendously popular hit. A third successful joint composition was "Charade" (1963).

Prior to their lucrative collaboration in the early 1960s, Mercer had been the lyricist or lyricist and composer for a long list of good songs, going back to the 1930s, and Mancini had created outstanding scores for the television series *Peter Gunn* (1958-1961) and *Mr. Lucky* (1959-1960) as well as notable scores for movies. So one of the great wordsmiths of the middle of the century and one of the best popular composers of the 1950s and 1960s got to pop the champagne cork together. A year after "Charade," Mancini by himself had another reason to celebrate due to another fine success. This time, though, it was probably pink champagne because the music involved was Mancini's delightful score for the first (1964) movie in the *Pink Panther* series.

Doctor Zhivago Theme

The United States had its bloody Civil War from 1861 to 1865. Russia had its even more devastating Revolution and Civil War from 1917 to 1921. In the U.S., the end of the conflict meant that the Union was preserved. In Russia, the end of the conflict meant that the Soviet Union was established.

Comparisons between the two landmark struggles do not stop there. Both major historical events have been portrayed in epic American motion pictures, and both of these motion pictures were enhanced by exceptional musical themes. For the U.S. Civil War the film classic was *Gone with the Wind* (1939), perhaps the best Hollywood movie ever produced, and the music was "Tara's Theme" or "My Own True Love." For the Russian Revolution, the film classic was *Doctor Zhivago* (1965), one of the best movies of its decade, and the music was "Lara's Theme" or "Somewhere My Love." Note that the titles "Tara's Theme" and "Lara's Theme" are identical except for the first letter, and that the variant titles both include the words "my" and "love."

Similarities continue. Both themes had no words in their original film premieres. Words for the *Wind* melody were added in 1954, and words for the *Zhivago* melody were added in 1966. Both lyricists, Mack David (1912-) for *Wind* and Paul Francis Webster (1907-1984) for *Zhivago*, also were involved with a number of other well-known songs. And finally, both rank among the very best film themes of all time.

But there are some differences, too. The music for *Wind* was created by an American, Max Steiner (1888-1971), while the music for *Zhivago* was created by a Frenchman, Maurice Jarre (1924-), a successful film composer. The *Zhivago* theme won an Oscar while the *Wind* theme did not. ("Over the Rainbow" was the winner that year.) Perhaps the biggest contrast, in conclusion, were the styles. "Tara's Theme" was dramatic and sweeping, while "Lara's

Theme" was soft and tender. Tara was a plantation, a symbol of a vanishing civilization. Lara was a young woman, the object of an ongoing love affair. The inspirations for the two songs varied markedly, and accordingly so did the end products.

Don't Fence Me In

If you have friends who think they are knowledgeable about music, try the following trivia puzzler on them. The cowboy ballad "Don't Fence Me In" was first sung by Roy Rogers in the 1944 movie *Hollywood Canteen*. Who was the composer?

Unless your friends are very sharp about the history of American popular music, they will not be able to come up with the correct answer. This very familiar western song, with the rhythm of a slowly moving horse, was actually composed by the very sophisticated easterner, Cole Porter. Yes, this is the same Cole Porter that wrote all those slick musicals with polished melodies and intricate lyrics. Porter (1891-1964) actually wrote the piece in the 1930s for a never-released film.

Although "Don't Fence Me In" may not be typical Porter, it does show touches of the Broadway master. The lyrics are subtly satirical, and the horse's hoofbeats suggest that the animal has had a bit of musical training.

Another trivia question you could pose concerns the 1945 motion picture *Don't Fence Me In* in which Rogers again sang the title song. What other famous western song was also in that movie, and who was the vocalist? The answer is "Tumbling Tumbleweeds" rendered by Gene Autry. ("Tumbleweeds" was written in 1934 by Bob Nolan.) Two other country-style songs popularized by Autry were "South of the Border, Down Mexico Way" (1939) by Jimmy Kennedy and Michael Carr, and "Mexicali Rose" (1923) with words by Helen Stone and music by Jack B. Tenny. Not to be outdone, Autry's cowboy associate Rogers also performed "Tumbleweeds" and "Mexicali Rose" in motion pictures.

Gigi

Lyricist Alan Jay Lerner (1918-1986) and composer Frederick Loewe (1904-1988) had never written songs for the movies prior to the 1958 musical film *Gigi*. But they had had plenty of practice on Broadway with *Brigadoon* (1947), *Paint Your Wagon* (1951), and *My Fair Lady* (1956). So when *Gigi* won the astounding total of nine Oscars, including best picture and best song, probably nobody was really surprised.

The score, featuring the very charming, bubbly bonbon of a title song, plus the tastily cute "Thank Heaven for Little Girls" performed as only Maurice Chevalier could, provided Lerner and Loewe yet another jewel in their crown of musical successes. After *Gigi* Lerner and Loewe were to have only one more major collaboration, the musical *Camelot* (1960), before they went their separate ways.

What they left behind, though, was about a quarter century of musical excellence. With a variety of songs emanating from five diverse periods and locales–medieval England, early twentieth century England, the West in the mid-nineteenth century, Scotland in the mid-twentieth century, and Paris anytime–Lerner and Loewe brought much pleasure to their generation and to at least one subsequent one. Technically, the story of *Gigi* was set in 1890s France, but romantic tales like the one in the film and pleasant ballads like "Gigi" are timeless in the city of light and love.

Gone with the Wind Theme

There can be little doubt as to which year was the greatest in American movie history. The eve of World War II, 1939, was a year of exceptional cinematographic triumphs. Among others, *The Wizard of Oz* and *Gone with the Wind* were produced in that very happy time for Hollywood. *Wizard* is perhaps the most charming and delightful movie of all time, and *Wind* is perhaps the most impressive. Both have been surrounded by an abundance of cult interest, attention in popular culture, and audience favor. Both are giant legends extending far beyond the movie screen.

Wind would probably rate as the most important film ever, and *Wizard* would also be a leading candidate. In one way, though, *Wizard* has surpassed the overall superior *Wind*. *Wizard*'s truly outstanding theme song, "Over the Rainbow" has had markedly more cultural impact than "Tara's Theme," the musical showpiece of *Wind*. But "Tara's Theme" is a very fine composition. With its sweep and sense of drama the song was a strong complement to the same characteristics in the plot and acting.

Composed by Max Steiner (1888-1971), "Tara's Theme" has become a major symbol of the film as a whole, the main characters Scarlett O'Hara and Rhett Butler, and the chief focus of the story, the plantation Tara. Fifteen years after the movie, in 1954, the melody's success led to the addition of lyrics by Mack David (1912-) and the creation of the song "My Own True Love." The words, although good, did not do a lot to enhance the reputation of "Tara's Theme" mainly because the melody seemed much more at home with Scarlett's home Tara than as a love ballad. Either with or without lyrics, it is a creditable piece, so frankly, my dear, I don't give a damn how it is performed.

Happy Days Are Here Again

This book will cover songs from A to Z. In a like manner the jubilant musical proclamation "Happy Days Are Here Again" covered authors from A to Y. That is, Milton Ager (1893-) wrote the music and Jack Yellen (1892-) wrote the words for the 1929 classic. Ager and Yellen also had other happy days with the highly successful toe tapper "Ain't She Sweet?" (1927) and the vaudeville favorite "Hard-Hearted Hannah" (1929). (Bob Bigelow and Charles Bates were co-lyricists for the latter.)

"Happy Days" was involved with a lot of borrowing. The tune and lyrics were not borrowed, but the title of the 1930 movie for which it was written, *Chasing Rainbows*, was obviously influenced by the title of the famous 1918 ballad "I'm Always Chasing Rainbows." (That song was created by lyricist Joseph McCarthy and composer Harry Carroll, with the melody borrowed from Frederic Chopin.) Later on, "Happy Days" apparently lent its title to the 1974-1984 comedy television series of the same name.

The most interesting borrowing, however, was by several Presidents, all Democrats. Franklin Roosevelt, Harry Truman, John Kennedy, and Lyndon Johnson all used the song in their campaigns or political activities. In effect, "Happy Days" has become the unofficial anthem for the Democratic Party. Wouldn't it be ironic if Ager and Yellen were actually Republicans?

Heigh, Ho

A half century or so after the appearance of Walt Disney's first full-length animated cartoon, *Snow White and the Seven Dwarfs* (1937), it is quite easy to sneer at the relative amateurishness of the production. Compared to later, more polished Disney masterpieces, *Snow White* seems to have been created by the bumbling talents of the seven dwarfs who were made famous by the film. Yet in its time, *Snow White* was a technological and entertainment marvel. It was a pioneer and as good as artistic groundbreaking ever gets.

The songs from *Snow White*, furthermore, remain a continuing part of American popular culture in spite of their not being especially good. In fact, "Some Day My Prince Will Come," "Whistle While You Work," and "Heigh, Ho" are all in a small way legends in our society, as well as the focus of jokes and satire. Lyricist Larry Morey and composer Frank Churchill surely never expected that their little ballads and ditties would still be well known, stereotypical, and even a bit controversial so many years after the movie's premiere.

"Some Day My Prince Will Come" has been targeted by feminists as an example of an unwise attitude for women. "Whistle While You Work" has become a cliché of the workplace. And the delightful lines "Heigh, ho, heigh, ho, It's off to work we go" have been turned into a parody on many occasions, for instance, a bumper sticker reading "I owe, I owe, So off to work I go." *Snow White* may not be the greatest musical of all time, but how many other films have such a charming and persistent three-pronged musical legacy?

The High and the Mighty

When Dmitri and Ned got together, the result frequently was dramatic, skillful songs about tough and rugged men. In the 1952 film *High Noon*, the pair portrayed the crisis of a Western lawman having a shootout with outlaws. In the 1959-1966 television western series *Rawhide*, Dmitri and Ned's stirring composition introduced the continuing saga of hard-working, hard-fighting cowboys taking herds of reluctant steers on the long trail to market. In the tense 1954 aviation movie *The High and the Mighty*, the duo produced the mighty good highlight of the outstanding film.

Dmitri Tiomkin (1894-1979) and Ned Washington (1901-1976) won Oscars for the scores of *High Noon* and *The High and the Mighty*. The haunting strains of "The High and the Mighty" theme song continue to inhabit airwaves and recordings many years after its introduction. Also called "The Whistling Song" because the film's star, John Wayne, whistled the tune throughout the production, the piece was even more spiritual and soulfully penetrating when performed that way.

It was probably the only time that high and mighty star "Duke" Wayne even whistled in a film, except to call his horse. When he was interested in a lady he never whistled at her. Instead, in direct and macho Wayne fashion, he just grabbed her.

High Hopes

A cartoon in the bizarre pictorial humor series "The Far Side" showed two women gloating because one of them had stepped on and killed an ant who was trying to get to a rubber tree plant in her house. The subtle reference to the 1959 song "High Hopes" would be lost to anybody who is not familiar with the entire composition. In one of the verses an ant with high hopes manages to move a rubber tree plant. The insect's accomplishment was also equaled by the exploits of "a silly old ram" who through persistence and a durable hard head was able to butt a dam into nonexistence.

This perpetually delightful and inspiring ballad was written by the famous wordsmith Sammy Cahn (1913-1992) and the almost as renowned musician James Van Heusen (1913-1990). Entirely consistent with the theme of the lyrics, the history of "High Hopes" demonstrates that even impromptu actions can achieve great things. When the 1959 non-musical film *A Hole in the Head* required an emotional, uplifting bit of music at the last minute, Cahn and Van Heusen quickly filled the need. This afterthought won an Academy Award and also resulted in one of the better recordings by Frank Sinatra (as if he needed another).

So the ant, the ram, Cahn, Van Heusen, and Sinatra all ended up on top because they all had high hopes for their various enterprises. The combination of fun, a good tune, and a positive message is what makes "High Hopes" so much more than the typical musical novelty.

High Noon

There's an old African or Asian expression about how only mad dogs and Englishmen stay out in the hot midday sun. In the outstanding 1952 western movie *High Noon*, there were no Englishmen present. But it could be said that the desperados trying to gun down the local peace officer in the middle of the day were as dangerous as mad dogs. In the end the bad guys ended up as dead dogs thanks to the bravery and gunfighting prowess of the lawman (Gary Cooper) and the unexpected last-minute armed intervention of his girlfriend (Grace Kelly).

Belted out magnificently by singer Frankie Laine in a best-selling recording which somewhat preceded the movie's release, the *High Noon* theme, or "Do Not Forsake Me," is one of several excellent collaborations by Ned Washington (1901-1976) and Dmitri Tiomkin (1894-1979). After their Academy Award-winning efforts with "High Noon," they repeated with another Oscar for "The High and the Mighty" (1954), and also co-created the splendid theme for the 1959-1966 TV series *Rawhide*.

Just as Gary Cooper's lady did not forsake him in the movie, listeners have not forsaken this emphatic pre-rock era ballad after almost two generations of screaming and gyrating youngsters (on stage and in the audience). The song, like the movie and the image of a shootout at high noon, is a classic, and classics, like bold marshals, do not die easily.

Jaws Theme

Huge marine animals have been key characters in several famous stories. There was the "great fish" (sometimes interpreted as a whale) that swallowed Jonah in the Old Testament, Moby Dick the white whale, the whale who tangled with Pinocchio, and the great white shark in the movie *Jaws* (1975). None of these creatures were particularly inclined to be friendly, but for pure ferociousness and meanness, the last-mentioned beast surpassed the rest.

One of the main nonaquatic features of the excellent original *Jaws* film, the good sequel "Jaws II" (1978), and the flop sequel *Jaws 3* (1983), was the unique, brilliant, pulsating, very memorable theme composed by John Williams. After receiving an Oscar for music direction in the 1971 movie *Fiddler on the Roof,* Williams (1932-) followed up with the same award for composing the scores for *Jaws* and *Star Wars* (1977). His creation of other good scores for *Close Encounters of the Third Kind* (1977), *Superman* (1978), *The Empire Strikes Back* (1980), *Raiders of the Lost Ark* (1981), *E.T., the Extraterrestrial* (1982), and *Return of the Jedi* (1983) collectively added up to the clear conclusion that Williams was the unchallenged master of movie music in the 1970s and 1980s.

Riding the wave of this long series of successes, Williams in 1980 changed his personal locale from Hollywood to Boston where he became director of the superlative Boston Pops Orchestra, succeeding the legendary Arthur Fiedler. In less than a decade, from Fiddler to Fiedler, Williams became one of the biggest fishes in the ocean of twentieth-century music.

Laura

Houses, castles, caves, trees, mountains, ships, and various other things have been said to be haunted. Supposedly, they are inhabited and controlled by ghosts and similar spirit phenomena.

If there ever was a motion picture that was haunted, it was the 1944 classic *Laura*. There were no ghosts, ghouls, or demons in the usual otherworldly sense. There was no intent to frighten or scare as in horror films. But there was a haunting psychological theme and a haunting portrait of the female lead, Gene Tierney, who played the role of Laura, a beautiful disturbed young woman. Most of all, there was the very haunting musical theme that over and over possessed the background.

At first, the sad and gorgeous melody by David Raksin (1912-) had no words. It really didn't need any, for its exquisite message of tragedy was very effectively communicated. Some time after the release of the film, in 1945, a set of words was added by the outstanding lyricist Johnny Mercer (1909-1976) in response to the tune's extensive popularity.

The words, though, were definitely secondary, since most recordings of "Laura" (and there have been many) are wordless. "Laura," incidentally, has haunted more American recording studios than almost any other composition except "Stardust." Two generations after the appearance of the moody movie, the sorrowful sounds of the song continue to capture us, penetrating long and deep into our very receptive psyches. This should be expected, for ghostly things never die.

Love Is a Many Splendored Thing

Perhaps the most insightful and sophisticated title for any love song was "Love Is a Many Splendored Thing." Those catching words by Paul Francis Webster (1907-1984), combined with a possessing melody by Sammy Fain (1902-1989), created the theme song of the compelling 1955 romantic film of the same name. The intensity of the lyrics matched the energy of the love affair, and the sweep of the music went well with the windswept hill in the Hong Kong locale. Webster and Fain won an Academy Award for the song, as well as for the 1953 ballad "Secret Love" from the film *Calamity Jane*. A third Webster-Fain concoction with "love" in the title was "April Love" (1957), which didn't earn any honors but sure made lots of money.

Lyricist Webster also collaborated on the songs "Lamplighter's Serenade" (1942) with Hoagy Carmichael, "The Loveliest Night of the Year" (1950) with Irving Aaronson, "Friendly Persuasion" (1956) with Dimitri Tiomkin, "The Twelfth of Never" (1956) with Jerry Livingston, the theme song for the television series *Maverick* (1958) with David Butolph, and "Shadow of Your Smile" (1965) with Johnny Mandel. This last song garnered both an Academy Award and a Grammy.

Composer Fain was similarly successful with other collaborators, including "That Old Feeling" (1937) with Lew Brown and "Dear Hearts and Gentle People" (1949) with Bob Hilliard, plus "Let a Smile Be Your Umbrella" (1927), "Wedding Bells Are Breaking Up That Old Gang of Mine" (1929), "I Can Dream, Can't I?" (1937), and "I'll Be Seeing You" (1938) with Irving Kahal. The last song was perhaps the biggest hit on the hit parade in 1944 and has been long associated with the career of Frank Sinatra.

This substantial list of Webster's and Fain's accomplishments clearly shows that talent, like love, can be a many splendored thing.

Lullaby of Broadway

Writing several successful songs does not ensure lasting fame. Take, for example, composer Harry Warren (1893-1981) and lyricist Al Dubin (1891-1945). Together and separately they produced a number of well-known popular pieces, but it is doubtful that the proverbial average American ever heard of them.

Their most famous joint composition was "Lullaby of Broadway," which won an Academy Award for its appearance in the 1935 movie musical *Gold Diggers of Broadway*. They also collaborated on "You're Getting to Be a Habit with Me" (1932), "Shuffle Off to Buffalo" (1932), "We're in the Money" (1933), "I Only Have Eyes for You" (1934), and "Lulu's Back in Town" (1935).

With lyricists other than Dubin, Warren created a similar list of songs. Mort Dixon and Billy Rose combined with Warren for "I Found a Million Dollar Baby" (1931), and Dixon and Joe Young combined with Warren for "You're My Everything" (1931). Mack Gordon and Warren co-authored "Chattanooga Choo Choo" (1941) and "You'll Never Know" (1943). With Johnny Mercer he wrote "Jeepers Creepers" (1938), "You Must Have Been a Beautiful Baby" (1938), and "On the Atchison, Topeka and the Santa Fe" (1945). Finally, he and Jack Brooks concocted "That's Amore" (1953), Dean Martin's popular "pizza pie" song.

Dubin with composer Joseph A. Burke wrote "Tip Toe Through the Tulips with Me" (1929), the ditty reintroduced on late 1960s television by the weird character "Tiny Tim," and "For You" (1930). With composer Burton Lane, Dubin created the charming novelty "Feudin' and Fightin'" (1944).

From the 1920s to the 1950s, Warren and Dubin contributed to a series of hits, some of which are quite good. They were even indirectly honored by the 1951 movie *Lullaby of Broadway*, which included the title song, "You're Getting to Be a Habit," and songs by other composers, for example, James F. Hanley's 1935 "Zing! Went the Strings of My Heart."

The Magnificent Seven Theme

With the glowing word "magnificent," plus lucky "seven," in the title, there was much to attract moviegoers to the 1960 western film *The Magnificent Seven.* With an excellent plot, several well-known and popular actors, plenty of gun fighting action, a clear victory of good over evil, and a brilliant musical score, there is much to keep viewers returning to the TV screen whenever this motion picture clasic is rerun and rerun and rerun.

The outstanding score–dramatic, pulsating, and compelling–was written by Bernstein. In this instance it was not Leonard, the famous composer, conductor, and television personality, but his lesser-known unrelated namesake Elmer (1922-). Although definitely overshadowed by the great Leonard, and not nearly as familiar to the American public as the cartoon character Elmer Fudd, the inept associate of Bugs Bunny, Elmer Bernstein nevertheless held his own when it came to cultural contributions. The composer of a long list of movie scores, including *The Man with the Golden Arm* (1955), *The Ten Commandments* (1956), *To Kill a Mockingbird* (1962), and *The Great Escape* (1963), Bernstein was one of Hollywood's most accomplished music men. His name may not be remembered by most of the public, but his creations, especially the sweeping theme of *The Magnificent Seven*, have been appreciated for over a generation. In that way he is similar to the other Bernstein and the other Elmer.

Mona Lisa

This is a tale of two persons who are household names and two who should be. The first celebrity, of course, is the world famous Mona Lisa, the wife of a Florentine merchant whose coy smile was immortalized in oil by the great painter and all-around genius Leonardo da Vinci. About four and a half centuries later, in 1949, Mona Lisa was perpetuated in a multi-million selling disk recording by one of the greatest vocal celebrities of all time, the fabulous Nat King Cole. Among the other top disks by Cole were "The Christmas Song" ("Chestnuts Roasting on an Open Fire"), written by Mel Tormé and Robert Wells in 1946, "Nature Boy," written by Eden Ahbez in 1946 and recorded in 1948, "Too Young" ("They tried to tell us we're too young"), written by Sylvia Dee and Sid Lippman in 1951, "Unforgettable," written by Irving Gordon in 1951, "Darling, Je Vous Aime Beaucoup," written by Anna Sosenko in 1935 and recorded in 1955, and "Ramblin' Rose" written by Joe and Noel Sherman in 1962.

Like the Mona Lisa in the painting, Cole also had a quite becoming and fetching smile. The composers of "Mona Lisa" almost surely smiled too, since they made a lot of money and earned several awards for their music. Yet unlike the beguiling Italian woman and the singer with the smooth, resonant tones, they are unknown to the average American. Jay Livingston (1915-) and Ray Evans (1915-) were one of the most successful songwriting teams of the 1940s and 1950s, but were by reputation strongly overshadowed by contemporary pairs like Rodgers and Hammerstein and Lerner and Loewe.

On top of Academy Award-winning "Mona Lisa," which in a fragmented Italian version was first introduced in the 1949 film nonentity *Captain Carey, U.S.A.*, Livingston and Evans wrote two other Academy Award songs. "Buttons and Bows" appeared in the Bob Hope and Jane Russell picture *The Paleface* (1948), and

"Whatever Will Be, Will Be" ("Que Sera, Sera") was introduced by Doris Day in Alfred Hitchcock's movie thriller *The Man Who Knew Too Much* (1956). (That song, along with "Everybody Loves a Lover" [1958], words by Richard Adler and music by Robert Allen, "Love Somebody" [1947] by Joan Whitney and Alex Kramer, and "Sentimental Journey" [1944] by Bud Green, Les Brown, and Ben Homer were standards in Day's fine repertory.) Add to these the well-known theme from the TV western series *Bonanza* (1959-1973), the exceptionally fine Christmas song "Silver Bells" (1951), plus other songs like "Tammy" (1957), and Livingston and Evans, or Jay and Ray, should be promptly inducted into the songwriting duo hall of fame, if there were one.

Moon River

M plus M eqauls MR. That was the artistic formula that created the already classic romantic composition "Moon River." M number one was the great lyricist Johnny Mercer (1909-1976). From the 1930s to the 1950s, Mercer in collaboration with various composers wrote the words for "Too Marvelous for Words" (1937), "Hooray for Hollywood" (1938), "You Must Have Been a Beautiful Baby" (1938), "Blues in the Night" (1941), "That Old Black Magic" (1942), "Tangerine" (1942), "Laura" (1945), "On the Atchison, Topeka, and the Santa Fe" (1945), "In the Cool, Cool, Cool of the Evening" (1951), "Glow-Worm" (1952), and "Autumn Leaves" (1955). By himself he also wrote the words and music for the amusing cowboy ballad "I'm an Old Cowhand" (1936) and the smooth love song "Dream" (1944). In addition, he popularized the whimsical "Zip-A-Dee-Doo-Dah" (1945), the Academy Award-winning composition by lyricist Ray Gilbert and composer Allie Wrubel, which originally appeared in Disney's 1946 film *Song of the South.*

Then in the early 1960s M number one started working with M number two, composer Henry Mancini. The talents of Mancini (1924-), already proven by very good television and movie scores, helped extend the productive career of Mercer with three joint songs. The first, and the best, was "Moon River," which was introduced in the 1961 movie *Breakfast at Tiffany's.* "MR" won an Oscar, two Grammys, and worldwide attention with at least a hundred different recordings. Mercer considered the lyrics to be his best ever, and singer Andy Williams, who crooned "MR" in the film, adopted the ballad as his theme song.

M and M also wrote "Days of Wine and Roses" from the 1962 film of that title, and "Charade," from the 1963 film of the same name. "W and R" exactly imitated "MR" by winning one Oscar and two Grammys, and being introduced by Williams. All three exceptional creations by the M and M team were sweet and succulent, like the chocolate candies using the same initials.

My Kind of Town

In 1989 the well-known lyricist Sammy Cahn (1913-1992) was specially brought to Chicago to be honored by that great midwestern community. Why did the "second city" show its appreciation for a person born in the "first city," New York? In part it may have been for his long and successful career that included the 1949 composition "Be My Love," authored with Nicholas Brodszky and magnificently bellowed by Mario Lanza on a two-million selling record, the 1945 classic "Let It Snow, Let It Snow, Let It Snow" and the 1954 Academy Award winner "Three Coins in a Fountain" with Jule Styne, and the award winners "Love and Marriage" (1955), "All the Way" (1957), "High Hopes" (1959), and "Call Me Irresponsible" (1963) with James Van Heusen.

Mostly, though, it was because of Cahn's collaboration with Van Heusen on their joint tribute to Chicago, "My Kind of Town." (Van Heusen (1913-1990) is also known by his real name, Edward Chester Babcock.) Introduced by Frank Sinatra in the 1964 musical movie *Robin and the Seven Hoods*, "My Kind of Town (Chicago Is)" has been, like the other four Cahn-Van Heusen songs, closely associated with Sinatra. It has also, of course, been closely associated with Chicago and has developed into the second theme of the second city, after the perpetual 1922 standard "Chicago" by Fred Fisher.

The song was also connected with another famous second. With parody words concocted by Cahn himself, "My Kind of Guy" was used in the 1964 senatorial campaign of Robert Kennedy, the second political Kennedy brother and, unfortunately, the second one to be killed by an assassin's bullets.

Our Love Is Here to Stay

The last piece of music by the great George Gershwin (1898-1937) was the memorable ballad "Our Love Is Here to Stay." It was left unfinished at Gershwin's premature death, but was completed by Vernon Duke. Ira Gershwin (1896-1983) added, as usual, a fine set of lyrics. In 1938 it was introduced in the motion picture *The Goldwyn Follies*.

The career of George and Ira could be described by "Our music is here to stay." So many good songs were crafted by the brother team, including "Bidin' My Time" (1930), "But Not for Me" (1930), "Embraceable You" (1930), "Fascinating Rhythm" (1924), "A Foggy Day" (1937), "I Got Plenty o' Nuthin'" (1935), "I Got Rhythm" (1930), "It Ain't Necessarily So" (1935), "I've Got a Crush on You" (1928), "Love Is Sweeping the Country" (1931), "Love Walked In" (1938), "The Man I Love" (1924), "Nice Work If You Can Get It" (1937), "Of Thee I Sing" (1931), "Oh, Lady Be Good" (1924), "'S Wonderful" (1927), "Someone to Watch Over Me" (1926), "Strike Up the Band!" (1930), "Summertime" (1935), and "They Can't Take That Away from Me" (1937).

George separate from Ira wrote "Somebody Loves Me" (1924) with lyricists Bud De Sylva and Ballard MacDonald, and "Swanee" (1919) with lyricist Irving Caesar. Ira with composer Harold Arlen wrote "The Man That Got Away" (1954).

In sentiment, "Our Love Is Here to Stay" is similar to Irving Berlin's "Always" (1925). It also, like "Always," is one of the composer's best pieces. Both songs, furthermore, were created when the composers were in the their late 30s. The one big difference, however, is that "Always" came in the first third of Berlin's career while "Our Love" came at the very end of Gershwin's.

Over the Rainbow

It was all quite improbable. The song had an unusual leap of an octave between the first and second notes. It was introduced by a relatively unknown teenager girl who was not especially pretty. The motion picture that featured the piece had production problems, had a plot that some people might consider silly, and had a scene where the screen changed quite awkwardly from black and white to full color. On top of all this, the song was three times deleted from the movie.

Yet "Over the Rainbow" not only survived being cut by the producers of *The Wizard of Oz* (1939), but managed to win the Academy Award and the hearts of millions of Americans. In 1963 it was selected as one of the 16 leading hits of the previous half century by the American Society of Composers, Authors, and Publishers (ASCAP). It was also the most famous song by composer Harold Arlen (1905-1986) and lyricist Edgar Yipsel Harburg (1898-1981). Arlen also wrote the music for "I've Got the World on a String" (1932), "Stormy Weather" (1933), "Blues in the Night" (1941), and "That Old Black Magic" (1942). Among Harburg's other lyrics were "April in Paris" (1932), "How Are Things in Glocca Morra?" (1947), and "Adrift on a Star" ("Here we are, Adrift on a star") (1961).

The movie was even a bigger winner. It launched the career of legendary Judy Garland, and became, eventually, perhaps the most beloved film of all time. The characters of Dorothy, Toto, the Scarecrow, the Tin Man, the Cowardly Lion, the Wizard, and the Wicked Witch of the West are among the most familiar of the twentieth century. The imaginary land of Oz and the real land of Kansas also became geographical celebrities. So much good and happiness has transpired because of this perpetually charming masterpiece of the silver screen and its wistful theme song that time after time have carried us "Over the Rainbow."

The Pink Panther Theme

In recent decades three specially colored panthers have come upon the American scene. There were the Black Panthers, a militant group of black young men, the Gray Panthers, a militant group of older persons, and the Pink Panther, who represented nothing but fun.

Starting with the film *The Pink Panther* in 1964, and followed by several movie sequels as well as a series of spinoff television cartoons, the pink non-serious variety of cat probably has had more affect on American life than has its two aggressive and serious cousins. With Peter Sellars masterfully portraying the bumbling, egotistical, and maddening French police detective who despite himself always managed to capture the culprit, accompanied by a delightful musical theme, the Pink Panther phenomenon has developed into a legend. The cartoon version of the panther and the theme have even been utilized for a long-running series of national television advertisements.

The pseudo-mysterious sounding, satirical "Pink Panther Theme" is perhaps the highlight of the career of Henry Mancini (1924-). For about ten years Mancini's skillful compositions kept him at the very top of the popular music mountain. In addition to the Panther movies, he also wrote the scores for *The Glenn Miller Story* (1954), *Breakfast at Tiffany's* (1961), *Days of Wine and Roses* (1962), *Charade* (1963) and other films, plus the fine themes for the television series *Peter Gunn* (1958-1961) and *Mr. Lucky* (1959-1960). His most famous song with lyrics attached is "Moon River," the dreamy ballad from *Breakfast at Tiffany's*.

Note that all the above-mentioned pieces of music, except one, are connected with sophisticated people and subjects. The one exception, of course, is the comedic "Pink Panther Theme," which will probably always be and should always be the musical partner of the classic buffonery of Chief Inspector Clouseau. The theme is about the only associate that the wild and dangerous crime-fighting antics of the inspector would not kill off or send to the madhouse.

Raindrops Keep Fallin' on My Head

For years, Bert and Ernie of Sesame Street were the delight of youngsters. Also for years, Burt and Hal of Tin Pan Alley were the delight of grownups.

Composer Burt Bacharach (1928-) and his lyricist partner Hal David wrote as many successful songs during the late 1950s, 1960s, and early 1970s as any other pair of pens. In 1958 came "Magic Moments," followed by "What the World Needs Now Is Love" in 1965 and "Alfie" in 1966. In 1968 the team had three hits; "Promises, Promises," "I'll Never Fall in Love Again," and "Do You Know the Way to San Jose?" The Carpenter's top recording, "Close to You," was written in 1970.

Possibly the best and most typical Bacharach-David composition was "Raindrops Keep Fallin' on My Head" (1970). A firm standard after only a generation, "Raindrops" has even gained the dubious status of elevator/telephone music. One thing not typical about the song, though, was its somewhat incongruous yet effective introduction in a western movie, *Butch Cassidy and the Sundance Kid*. Not only did raindrops fall on Cassidy and Sundance's heads during the course of the story, gaining an Academy Award for Bacharach and David, but at the end of the film a hailstorm of bullets fell upon the two outlaws from head to toe. Bacharach and David, however, did not produce any appropriate music for the final non-magic moments of the desperados. ("Stormy Weather" had already been written.)

Rocky's Theme

"Stallone" is the Italian word for "stallion," and the most famous roles played by the well-known movie actor Sylvester Stallone completely lived up to that description. In *First Blood* (1982), Stallone portrayed Rambo, a virile and resourceful army veteran who survived in the wild while being pursued by a host of armed men. In *Rocky* (1976) and its sequels, he was a tough, gritty boxer who overcame all obstacles. So for "S. S.," "R and R" did not mean the recuperative powers of rest and relaxation, but the considerable physical powers of *Rambo* and *Rocky*.

The tale of Rambo was visually enhanced by the rugged scenery of the Pacific Northwest. The saga of Rocky was acoustically enhanced by an exhilarating musical theme. Also known as "Gonna Fly Now," "Rocky's Theme" was composed by Bill Conti, who also did the scores for *Harry and Tonto* (1974), *An Unmarried Woman* (1978), *The Karate Kid* (1984), and other films. The lyrics were by Ayn Robbins and Carol Connors, but usually the words are deleted in favor of the rousing and dynamic instrumental version, which in relatively few years has developed into a solid, often performed standard. The character was named *Rocky* and the path of his life was often the same, but there is nothing rocky about the quality and success of this first-rate theme.

Singin' in the Rain

The old expression "He doesn't know enough to get out of the rain" applied to Gene Kelly in the 1952 movie *Singin' in the Rain.* Floating on a shower of romance, master dancer Kelly gracefully romped through and around city puddles while gleefully singing "Singin'." The long, wet sequence was one of the most memorable musical occasions in motion picture history. Among the few that surpassed it was Kelly's fantastic multi-scene ballet enterprise to end the 1951 film *An American in Paris.*

But Gene was not the first Kelly to perform "Singin' in the Rain" in a movie. *Little Nellie Kelly,* also known as Judy Garland, sang it in the 1940 film musical of that name. And eleven years earlier a non-Kelly, Cliff Edwards, introduced the ballad in another screen musical, *Hollywood Revue of 1929.* In 1929 "Singin'" was just part of the score, by 1940 it was special enough to be added to the production, and by 1952 it was the title piece and musical focus of the excellent motion picture.

"Singin'" was written by the songwriting team of lyricist Arthur Freed (1894-1973) and composer Nacio Herb Brown (1896-1964). Their collaboration was not the most successful of all time, and yet they did produce some good songs. Among their best were "All I Do Is Dream of You" (1934), "My Lucky Star" (or "You Are My Lucky Star") (1935), and "You Were Meant for Me" (1929), all of which were included in the 1952 movie. Perhaps their finest work was "Temptation," which propelled the career of Bing Crosby in the 1933 movie *Going Hollywood.*

Brown separate from Freed also created "You're an Old Smoothie" (1932) with lyricist Bud De Sylva and co-composer Richard A. Whiting, and "You Stepped Out of a Dream" (1940) with lyricist Gus Kahn. Brown with and without Freed came up with some memorable compositions, but most striking of all had the unforgettable first name "Nacio," which is Spanish for "I am born." Brown's parents apparently had the same creative streak as their talented son.

Star Wars Theme

John Williams is an ordinary and everyday name. But John Williams (1932-) the film composer and director of the Boston Pops Orchestra is far from an ordinary and everyday person. With three Academy Awards and widespread acclaim for his work in motion picture music, he is one of the leading artistic figures of the late twentieth century.

In contrast with his prosaic and mundane name, the movies for which he created scores tended to deal with science fiction or fantasy themes. *Star Wars* (1977) and its two sequels *The Empire Strikes Back* (1980) and *Return of the Jedi* (1983), as well as *Close Encounters of the Third Kind* (1977) and *E.T., the Extraterrestrial* (1982), all dealt with space travel. *Jaws* (1975), *Superman* (1978), and *Raiders of the Lost Ark* (1981) all focused on the unreal. The bizarre and adventuresome nature of these films causes one to ask if Williams could as effectively compose for more commonplace plots. He probably could, since his direction of the music (but not the composition of the songs) for the 1971 movie *Fiddler on the Roof* won him an Oscar. One suspects, however, that Williams would be at his best with the spectacular and the unusual.

Williams' other Oscars came for *Jaws* and *Star Wars*. His bold and expansive music for the latter is a major component of the cult attention given to the film. The score was as essential to the overall impact of the production as were the characters Luke Skywalker and Darth Vader. Like the themes for *Jaws* and to a lesser extent *Superman*, the music for *Star Wars*, in the public's eye, cannot be readily disassociated from the rest of this already legendary Hollywood classic.

Stayin' Alive

They called themselves the Bee Gees because of the initials of their leader, Barry Gibb. "BG" also could have meant "Better Group," since the Bee Gees were certainly one of the superior popular groups of the late 1970s and early 1980s.

The Bee Gee's biggest triumph, probably, was in the 1977 movie *Saturday Night Fever.* Barry, Robin, and Maurice Gibb sang several of their own songs as background music for the film that epitomized the disco craze of the time. Among the songs were the pulsating dance piece "Night Fever," the fine love ballad "How Deep Is Your Love?" (which won the Ivor Novello Award), and "Stayin' Alive." The last song is an excellent rock composition that not only captured the essence of disco but had enough substance and touches of imagination to survive long after disco had gone down the drain. "Stayin' Alive" has even been inserted into the repertory of elevator music, a perhaps questionable choice to anyone with a fear of elevators. Also in the film was the 1976 phenomenon "Disco Duck" by Rick Dees, which perhaps was the most representative song of the cultural blip called disco.

It's curious that three of the most creative male rock groups began with the letter "B" ("Bee Gees," "Beach Boys," and "Beatles.") The Rolling Stones also wrote much of their own material, and certainly have attained their share of notoriety, but it is this author's opinion that none of the Rolling Stones' songs have gathered enough mainstream cultural moss to be included in this volume.

That Old Black Magic

The analogy of love being magic and casting spells is an old one. Yet that theme has not appeared often in American popular music. On the several occasions when magic and witchery have conjured up a song, the best-known results were "Bewitched, Bothered and Bewildered" (1940), words by Lorenz Hart and music by Richard Rodgers, "That Old Black Magic" (from the 1942 movie *Star-Spangled Rhythm*), words by Johnny Mercer and music by Harold Arlen, "It's Magic" (1948), words by Sammy Cahn and music by Jule Styne, and "Witchcraft" (1957), words by Carolyn Leigh and music by Cy Coleman. Note that with the exception of the last one, this magic quartet was charmed by outstanding songwriting sorcerers.

Warlocks Arlen (1905-1986) and Mercer (1909-1976) combined their creative powers a few other times during the 1940s. "Blues in the Night" (1941), "One for My Baby" (1943), "Ac-cent-tchuate the Positive" (1944), and "Come Rain or Come Shine" (1946) captivated the attention of the mortals. "Blues," one of the best such numbers ever written, and "Black Magic," with superlative compelling lyrics and an appropriately mysterious-sounding melody, were definite masterpieces of the Arlen-Mercer brew. Even during the spells when they conspired with other artists, or worked alone, their rate of success was spooky. It didn't seem to matter that their collaborator might be a less-accomplished person, for example, when Mercer produced "Tangerine" in 1942 with little-known composer Victor Schertzinger. The spirit of triumph was almost always there.

There is one matter yet unresolved in this tale. Was it magic or talent that allowed the "Black" and "Blues" song-making duo to go down in history with their reputations unbruised?

The Third Man Theme

Vienna has been the locale for the creation of a tremendous body of waltzes and other fine music. Vienna was also the locale for the tremendous motion picture *The Third Man* (1950), a classic British spy thriller. The theme from the film was also Viennese in spirit, for it utilized the subdued chords of the zither, a favorite central European instrument.

Anton Karas, the composer of "The Third Man Theme," extracted the inspiration for his excellent instrumental from an eight measure melody discovered in a volume of zither music. From that modest scrap Karas developed one of the finest movie themes ever, and one suitable for the outstanding production. The pairing of the soft, folkish strains of the background music with the tense drama of the plot was a stroke of genius.

Another outstanding movie theme of the same period was "Unchained Melody" from the 1955 film *Unchained*. Written by lyricist Hy Zaret and composer Alex North, "Unchained Melody" has become a standard, particularly in instrumental versions with full orchestra. A third notable mid-century movie theme, "Intermezzo," from the 1941 film of that name, is similarly typically performed with substantial instrumentation. (Robert Henning wrote the words and Heinz Provost created the music.)

In contrast, "The Third Man Theme" is usually performed solo on the zither, including when used as the theme for a radio series derived from the movie. "The Third Man Theme's" high-pitched tones and gentle spirit were also in sharp opposition to the deep voice and unsettling stage personality of actor Orson Welles who starred in both the motion picture and radio versions.

Three Coins in a Fountain

Throwing coins into a fountain is supposed to bring good luck. It is uncertain whether this act has ever directly resulted in an improvement of fortunes, but the people who gather the money from the bottom of the fountains certainly are better-off financially.

The fountain mentioned in the Oscar-winning 1954 ballad "Three Coins in a Fountain" was the Fountain of the Trevi in Rome. That very historic city was the setting for the motion picture with the same name as the song. After the appearance of the film, the fountain, with its legend that whoever puts a coin into the water has to come back to the city, became a major lure for tourists and their money. During this period, coin-retrieving activity from Trevi was no doubt a very lucrative activity.

So was songwriting if you had the talent of wordsmith Sammy Cahn (1913-) and tunesmith Jule Styne (1905-). Among other songs, Cahn and Styne co-created "Saturday Night Is the Loneliest Night in the Week" (1944), "Let It Snow, Let It Snow, Let It Snow" (1945), "It's Been a Long, Long Time" (1945), "Five Minutes More" (1946), "It's Magic" (1948), and "Three Coins." And they both had hits with other collaborators. For example, Cahn wrote "Teach Me Tonight" (1954) with composer Gene DePaul, and Styne wrote the Grammy Award-winning "People" (1964) with lyricist Bob Merrill. Perhaps Cahn and Styne in their youth both threw three coins in their local fountains.

Where the Blue of the Night Meets the Gold of the Day

During his tremendous career as a singer, Harry "Bing" Crosby (1904-1977) popularized a wide variety of compositions. His recordings ranged from the comedy novelty "Pistol Packin' Mama" (1943) by Al Dexter to the splendid holiday classic "White Christmas" (1942) by Irving Berlin.

On top of his singing, acting, and comedy work he even did a bit of composing. In collaboration with Roy Turk (1892-1949), he created the lyrics for "Where the Blue of the Night Meets the Gold of the Day." (The title was long enough to require two lyricists!) Coupled with a melody by Fred E. Ahlert (1892-1953), "Where the Blue" was introduced by Crosby in the 1931 film *The Big Broadcast.* The movie not only provided Crosby with his theme song, but also his first starring screen role.

Turk and Ahlert never again had a more illustrious collaborator, yet they did contribute to some equally good ballads. Turk created "Walkin' My Baby Back Home" (1930) with Ahlert and Harry Richman, wrote the words for "Are You Lonesome Tonight?" (1926) to music by Lou Handman, and with Jack Smith wrote the words for "Gimme a Little Kiss, Will Ya, Huh?" (1926) to music by Maceo Pinkard. Ahlert created the tune for "I'm Gonna Sit Right Down and Write Myself a Letter" (1935) to accompany Joe Young's lyrics and the tune for "The Moon Was Yellow" (1934) to go with Edgar Leslie's lyrics.

Turk and Ahlert were not brilliant artists, but to some extent they were a generation ahead of their time. Three of their compositions were very successfully revived in the 1950s and 1960s. "Walkin' My Baby" was recorded by Johnnie Ray in 1952, "I'm Gonna Sit" by Billy Williams in 1956, and "Are You Lonesome" by Elvis Presley in 1960.

You Are My Sunshine

The moon gets most of the publicity in music. Compared to that mere reflection of solar rays, the mighty sun, the source of all life on earth, plus other stars have gotten relatively little attention from songwriters. There was however the upbeat 1940 ballad "You Are My Sunshine" by Jimmie Davis and Charles Mitchell. Introduced in the movie *Take Me Back to Oklahoma*, "Sunshine" has become a country/western standard.

Other bright sun songs were "Sunny" (1925) by lyricists Otto Harbach and Oscar Hammerstein II and composer Jerome Kern, "Sunny Side Up" (1929) by lyricists Bud De Sylva and Lew Brown and composer Ray Henderson, "Sunrise Serenade" (1939) by lyricist Jack Lawrence and composer Franke Carle, "That Lucky Old Sun" (1949) by lyricist Haven Gillespie and composer Beasley Smith, "Sunrise, Sunset" (1964) by lyricist Sheldon Harnick and composer Jerry Bock, and "Sun in the Mornin' and the Moon at Night" (1946) by Irving Berlin. Note that the moon got the last word in the Berlin song.

Star songs about stars have included "Starlight" (1931) by lyricist Joe Young and composer Bernice Petkere; "Adrift on a Star" (1961) with lyrics by Edgar Yipsel Harburg attached to Jacques Offenbach's "Barcarolle"; Catch a Falling Star" (1958) by Paul J. Vance and Lee Pockriss; "My Lucky Star" (1935) by lyricist Arthur Freed and composer Nacio Herb Brown; "Don't Let the Stars Get in Your Eyes" (1952) by Slim Willet, Cactus Pryor, and Barbara Trammel; "Stars Fell on Alabama" (1934) by lyricist Mitchell Parish and composer Frank Perkins; and "Swinging on a Star" (1944) by lyricist Johnny Burke and composer James Van Heusen.

The brightest star in all of popular music, clearly, was "Stardust" (1927) by lyricist Parish and composer Hoagy Carmichael. The moon as a musical theme may outnumber the sun and other stars, but the shiniest object in twentieth-century space is a piece from the sparkling star minority.

TELEVISION

All in the Family Theme

If you and millions of others had judged the long-running TV series *All in the Family* exclusively on its opening theme, the show would have been very short running. First of all, the melody is not exceptional or even particularly memorable. Second, the performance of the song by the characters Archie and Edith Bunker certainly could not by any stretch of semantics be called highly artistic. But remember that this was a comedy with conflicting and incongruous personalities and situations. Therefore, the off-key, amateurish rendering by the couple was completely at home in the amusingly turbulent environment of the Bunker household. Third, there was some trouble with understanding the lyrics and until the song was re-recorded with the next-to-last line very carefully enunciated by the singers, few people knew that the words in question were "Gee, our old LaSalle ran great."

Nevertheless, because of the fame and popularity of the 1971-1983 series, the old-fashioned style theme "Those Were the Days" by Strouse and Adams became famous too. It wasn't a great composition, but it introduced one of television's greatest comedies. Very effectively blending humor and social issues, *All in the Family* altered the course of television history. Subsequently, just about any topic was deemed appropriate for viewing on the tube.

When the format of the program was rearranged in 1979, shifting the setting to a bar, changing the show's title to *Archie Bunker's Place*, and phasing out the character of Edith, the theme also was tinkered with. With the decreasing emphasis on Edith, it was felt that Archie's and her singing of the theme was no longer suitable. So an instrumental version was substituted, thus eliminating the slightly embarrassing but eminently charming duet that added so much distinctiveness and flavor to the show.

Batman Theme

Batman has been a sensation of American popular culture three different times in the half century since the cartoon character was created by Bob Kane in 1939. In the 1940s and 1950s the printed exploits of Batman and Robin were beloved entertainment for both children and adults. In 1966 the comedy adventure series *Batman* erupted onto television screens with a "Pow" and a "Bang," like the animated words superimposed over the action during fights between the good guys and the bad guys. A little over two years later, the absurd crime-fighting activities of the Dynamic Duo were no longer the delight of campy television audiences, and the show quietly left the airwaves in 1968. Cartoon spinoffs and inane parodies like "Jingle Bells, Batman Smells" appeared during the 1970s, but the Batman rage seemed to be effectively gone with the demise of the short-lived but high impact series starring Adam West and Burt Ward.

Then in 1989 Batman again leaped into the forefront of things trendy with the premiere of the movie of the same name. The *Batman* movie was Robin-less and much heavier in mood. The succession of versions leads us to ask: Which is the real Batman–the straightforward hero of the forties, the burlesque figure of the sixties, or the darker character of the eighties? Surely not the last, and probably not the middle one.

One of the more interesting features of the 1960s TV show was the lively, freewheeling, and somewhat singsong musical theme. It certainly was not a great composition, but did match the broad spoof atmosphere of the plots. And it definitely was not the heftiest accomplishment of respected bandleader Neal Hefti (1922-), but because of the Batman craze may be the one most familiar to the American public.

Bonanza Theme

Bonanza was a true bonanza for its producers and stars. The long-running horse opera, which chronicled the action and human interest adventures of the Cartwrights in Virginia City, Nevada, was a strong favorite from 1959 to 1973. Only *Gunsmoke* exceeded the longevity and success of *Bonanza* as a television western series.

The composers of the theme from *Bonanza* had a similar success too, but with some differences. There were four Cartwrights roaming the Ponderosa, while only two songwriters created the song. The actors in the series were made international celebrities by those roles, while the theme makers were already famous in the popular music world when *Bonanza* galloped into American households.

Jay Livingston (1915-) and Ray Evans (1915-) collaborated on no less than three Academy Award winners, "Buttons and Bows" (1948), "Mona Lisa" (1949), and "Whatever Will Be, Will Be" or "Que Sera, Sera" (1956). They also produced the great pop Christmas classic "Silver Bells" (1951). So by the time Livingston and Evans wrote the hard-riding theme for *Bonanza*, they both had carved several big notches on their artistic guns.

Cheers Theme

Bars had been successfully employed as settings for mass media entertainment prior to the 1982 premiere of *Cheers.* But who would have thought that a comedy series about a collection of semi-misfits and life's irregulars working in or inhabiting your friendly neighborhood watering hole would not only be a hit in the ratings but offer something for the intellect?

Led by ladies' man Sam and pseudo-intellectual Diane constantly at love and war with each other, and supported by bartenders Coach and Woody (both lacking something upstairs), sarcastic waitress Carla, obnoxious mailman Cliff, unambitious accountant Norm, insecure psychologist Frasier, and the generally out-of-step bar manager Rebecca, *Cheers* consistently served up a beer barrel of laughs liberally interjected with poignancy.

One of the many ingredients that made *Cheers* an extraordinary brew is the simple but effective theme, "Where Everybody Knows Your Name," which subtly and gently led into each episode. Written by Judy Hart Angelo and Gary Portnoy, the song was an interesting contrast to the frequently abrasive, disruptive, and confusing atmosphere in the *Cheers* bar. The musical restraint in the ballad was so different from the conflict and chaos that normally followed, that it intentionally or unintentionally added one more layer of class to the TV classic. The *Cheers* parade of beers, fears, tears, leers, sneers, jeers, dears, and peers also had something for the ears.

Dragnet Theme

There is little doubt about what is the best-known and most successful police show in television history. With its realism, meticulous detail, and the low-key narration by creator Jack Webb, who starred as the stone-faced Sgt. Joe Friday, *Dragnet* remains the epitome of "cops and robbers" dramas.

The TV series, which began on radio in 1949, ran from 1951 to 1959 and was revived again from 1967 to 1970. The high popularity and longevity of the show was bolstered by the banging of the symbolic hammer of justice at the end of each episode and by its famous theme music. Known as "Dragnet March" or "Danger Ahead," it was written by pop composer and choral conductor Walter Schumann (1913-1958), who should not be confused with the better-known musicians Robert Schumann, a nineteenth-century German classical master, and William Schuman (one "n"), a noted twentieth-century American composer.

Dragnet's attention-getting four-note beginning, "Dum-de-dum-dum," underscored the serious crime matters that were about to be reenacted. (A similar very effective four-note introduction to drama is also present in Beethoven's superlative fifth symphony.) The theme and the program were such big hits that in 1953, less than two years after their television premiere, they both were honored by an extraordinary parody. Stan Freberg's hilarious million-selling recording, "St. George and the Dragonet," using Schumann's music, became number one on the hit parade. The situation of a television program and its parody both hitting the top is probably unique in American cultural history.

This essay, which contained only the facts ma'am, was written on a Friday (really). No names were changed to protect the innocent because all persons involved were guilty of excellence.

The George Burns and Gracie Allen Show Theme

Cigar-smoking, unflappable George Burns and well-intentioned, addled Gracie Allen kept audiences laughing for decades. From vaudeville through a long-running radio series in the 1930s and 1940s to their TV series of 1950-1958, Gracie's antics and the predicaments she created counterbalanced by the calm and philosophical personality of husband George added up to one of the most successful comedy formulas ever. George was always the straight man, with one exception. When otherwise sensible George yielded to the illusion that he was a great singer, the roles were reversed and Gracie actually became, temporarily, the wiser one.

The music that introduced George and Gracie for many years on radio and television was, appropriately, "Love Nest," by composer Louis A. Hirsch (1887-1924) and lyricist Otto Harbach (1873-1963). "Love Nest," from the 1920 musical *Mary*, was Hirsch's most famous melody because of its association with Burns and Allen beginning in the 1940s. Harbach (originally Hauerbach) wrote the lyrics for many other well-known songs, including "Love is Like a Firefly" (1912), "Indian Love Call" (1924), "Rose Marie" (1924), "I Won't Dance" (1935), and "Smoke Gets in Your Eyes" (1933).

But as George, stogie in hand, might have commented, "Otto who? Lou Hirsch wrote the tune, that's all we used, that's all we need to know." Puff, puff. End of monologue.

Gunsmoke Theme

Gunsmoke, the chemical residue of a discharged firearm, only lasts a few seconds. The television program named after this wispy, short-lived phenomenon, on the other gun hand, lasted quite a lot longer. The brief, tense, fast-draw confrontation between tough Marshall Matt Dillon and a nameless bad guy, which emphatically introduced each episode, was seen for 20 years, from 1955 to 1975. The most successful TV western of all time, it originally aired as a radio series in 1952. When transferred to the small screen (filled completely by the massive six-foot-seven frame of star James Arness), it helped spawn a big herd of TV westerns over the next decade, all of which were buried in video boot hill prior to the demise of *Gunsmoke*.

Set in Dodge City, Kansas, around 1880, *Gunsmoke* was a classic of good over evil, justice over lawlessness, and truth over dishonesty. As Marshall Dillon himself stated, he was not the quickest gun in the west, but he was a very straight shooter. Supported by his long-term associates, Doc, Kitty, Chester, Festus, and others, Dillon with his entertaining sagas helped pacify both the plains and the public of the U.S.

In light of the sweep and impact of *Gunsmoke*, its musical theme, known as "Old Trails," seems almost lost in the 20 years of gunfights and trail dust. It's a good theme, and certainly very familiar, but the composition by Glenn Spencer and Rex Koury provides more of a musical background or mood than a centerpiece for the show. But in the format of *Gunsmoke*, with only one real star, the subordinate role of the theme blends in quite well.

Hawaii Five-O Theme

What made *Hawaii Five-O* the longest-running police series in television history? Sure, the exploits of Steve McGarrett and his associates in the special unit of the Hawaiian State Police were consistently entertaining. Sure, the plots and characters wore well on audiences. Sure, the underlying theme was the age-old motif of good over evil. But there must be an additional explanation for the considerable success of the 1968-1980 program.

The answer to this inquiry appears dramatically at the very beginning of each show. The gigantic blue wave surging toward the beach at Waikiki (or whatever location) is a watery symbol of the series' appeal. In other words, it was the magnificent scenery of Hawaii, in tandem with well-done episodes, that kept *Hawaii Five-O* on the air for well over a decade. People who had never been to the islands could delight in the glimpses of paradise. People who had been there could revel in the memories of the special trip.

In addition to all of this, the program had an excellent theme composed by Mort Stevens. Erupting onto the screen at the exact same moment as the crest of the wave, the combination of strong sound and potent picture could make one tingle, even be overwhelmed in a very pleasant way. The music was the brilliant whitecap that topped off a 12-year weekly visit to our lovely fiftieth state.

Hill Street Blues Theme

Composer Mike Post was in an artistic rut during the 1970s and 1980s. Time after time he would come up with good scores for popular, long-running TV series, usually associated with detective/police/law dramas. Included in such music were the themes for *The Rockford Files* (1974-1980), *Magnum, P.I.* (1980-1988), *L. A. Law* (1986-), and, best of all, *Hill Street Blues* (1981-1987).

The *Hill Street Blues* theme is a sensitive, reflective jazz composition with a definite debt to classical music. It is one of the relatively few television themes that are frequently played in a non-television context. Post's outstanding score matched up well with the outstanding scripts and acting of the show, which were sensitive and reflective with clear touches of humor. Set in a fictional ghetto police station in an unnamed city (obviously intended to be Chicago), *Hill Street* realistically portrayed the everyday activities of the men and women of the precinct. Everything imaginable was covered–triumphs, tragedies, strengths, weaknesses, beautiful moments, and ugly incidents.

The title *Hill Street Blues* contains a triple-meaning pun. Blue was the color of the police uniforms. Blue was the dominating mood of the officers struggling in the difficult crime environment. And blue was the style of Mike Post's fine musical accompaniment to the scenarios of Hill Street.

I Love Lucy Show Theme

You could argue whether Milton Berle, Jackie Gleason, Red Skelton, or even Ernie Kovacs was the king of comedy on early television. But there would be no dispute as to who was the queen of TV humor, and that of course was the wacky redhead, Lucille Ball. Whether in the original 1951-1957 series, *I Love Lucy*, the 1962-1974 series *The Lucy Show*, or the various full-hour specials, Lucy was loved by millions and still is.

Even her stint on Broadway worked out well. In the 1960 musical *Wildcat*, Lucy commanded "Hey, Look Me Over," by lyricist Carolyn Leigh and composer Cy Coleman, a totally unnecessary request in light of her extensive popularity.

Lucy was great but received plenty of good help from excellent scripts and a fine supporting cast in the original series and the specials. Involved in or reacting to Lucy Ricardo's dizzy schemes were real-life husband Desi Arnaz as spouse Ricky Ricardo and Vivian Vance and William Frawley as the Mertzes. Also adding to the success of the *Lucy* shows was the lively, Latin American-beat theme "I Love Lucy," written by Harold Adamson (1906-) and Eliot Daniel. (Adamson also was the lyricist for "Around the World," the theme of the 1956 movie *Around the World in Eighty Days*, and for the standard ballad "Time on My Hands" (1930).

The *Lucy* song produced in audiences the same type of conditioned response as Pavlov's experiments did with his famous dogs. When the bouncy strains of Lucy's theme hit the air, millions took to their seats to routinely receive the reward of a hilarious session of comedy.

The Jack Benny Show Theme

Jack Benny had a highly popular, long-lived television comedy series from 1950 to 1965. Yet he belonged more to radio where he had been a network regular since 1932. When he transferred his low-key, understated routines to television, he brought along with him the beloved Benny gang of supporting cast members. Eddie "Rochester" Anderson, Mary Livingston, Don Wilson, Dennis Day, and Mel "Bugs Bunny" Blanc all became household names because of the program, and Frank Nelson's impertinent tones and lines like the drawn out "Yes?" made at least his voice and personality very familiar to listeners.

Benny also took his radio theme, "Love in Bloom," into TV-tube land. Composer Ralph Rainger (1901-1942) and lyricist Leo Robin (1900-) originally wrote the song for the 1934 motion picture *She Loves Me Not.* A rising young crooner named Bing Crosby capably introduced the polished, high-class ballad in the film. It was the Benny show, though, that made the piece a fixture in American culture.

Rainger and Robin (they sound like a mixup between *The Lone Ranger* and *Batman*) also collaborated on other notable songs, such as "June in January" (1934), "Blue Hawaii" (1937), and "Thanks for the Memory" (1937). Bob Hope adopted the last-mentioned composition as his perpetual theme song. You mathematicians–what are the odds that two out of America's three most beloved and enduring comedians (the other is George Burns) would have chosen as their lifelong themes pieces from the same duo of songwriters?

The Jackie Gleason Show Theme

He was called "the great one," an epithet that was quite appropriate. His corpulent, rotund figure was part of the reason for that sizable description, but at least as much was because of over 20 years as one of the very top comedians on television. Starting with *The Cavalcade of Stars* in 1950, and continuing until 1971 (with some interruptions), Jackie Gleason was a standout TV personality. Whether as host of "The Jackie Gleason Show," with his favorite expressions "And away we go" and "How sweet it is," or as the main character in *The Honeymooners* proclaiming "To the moon, Alice" and "Alice, you're the greatest," he became a big legend of the little screen.

In addition to his versatility as a comedian, with his roles as the Poor Soul, Joe the Bartender, Ralph Kramden, and several others, Gleason (1916-1987) was also a musician of some talent. He was an orchestra conductor who produced a number of pleasant, soft recordings, as well as a composer who wrote, among other pieces, the theme for his own show. The pensively expansive yet sweet and smooth bars of the music that introduced *The Honeymooners* and most of the telecasts of *The Jackie Gleason Show* were written in 1953. Entitled "Melancholy Serenade," an interesting contrast to the overall non-melancholy nature of his shows, the theme became the trademark or low-key fanfare for Gleason. This suggests that perhaps the true essence of Gleason was not the unabashed buffoon on center stage but instead the reserved artist behind the gentle baton.

The Lawrence Welk Show Theme

Critics called it "square," "corny," and "old-fashioned." Historians could describe it as "popular," "enduring," and "successful." No matter how you may characterize *The Lawrence Welk Show,* it was on the air for an amazing 27 years (network TV from 1955 to 1971, and syndication from 1971 to 1982). With maestro Welk holding a tight rein over his "family," the singers and orchestra performed straightforward traditional style music to the delight of millions. Welk's program pleased viewers but he never seemed very comfortable on camera even after many years and though born in the U.S., never quite mastered English pronunciation.

Just as conventional and sentimental as the rest of the show was the famous theme "Bubbles in the Wine." Written by Welk (1903-1992), the famous composer and lyricist Frank Loesser (1910-1969), and Bob Calame, the light, fluffy, melodic waltz became the trademark of the maestro of Saturday night. Along with Welk's awkward accent and the champagne bubbles which appeared on the screen, the bouncy piece was the target of jokes and parodies. One particular parody poked fun at all three, and by doing so probably confirmed that they all had become minor institutions of American popular culture. In the parody, Welk couldn't turn off the bubble machine, and it continued to generate bubbles indefinitely. In real life, Welk managed to turn on a loyal and sizable audience and for a while it seemed as if his show would go on indefinitely.

M*A*S*H Theme

One of the liveliest motion picture titles of all time was *The Russians Are Coming, the Russians Are Coming*, a delightful 1966 comedy about the Cold War coming to Maine. One of the dreariest song titles of all time was "Suicide Is Painless," the theme song for the outstanding 1972-1983 television comedy series, *M*A*S*H*. That classic show chronicled the humorous escapades and poignant moments of everyday operations in the 4077th Mobile Army Surgical Hospital in the Korean conflict of 1950-1953. A blend of comedic situations and social issues, *M*A*S*H* offered such a strong array of amusing characters, led by Dr. Benjamin Franklin Pierce ("Hawkeye"), that viewers almost forgot that the 4077th was only an oasis in a time of death and suffering. In complete harmony with the unconventional nature of the show, incidentally, were the satirical lyrics for "Suicide is Painless," written by Mike Altman, which were never used on the program.

Based on the hit 1970 movie of identical title, *M*A*S*H* became indirectly linked with the controversial Vietnam War, which was still very much on the minds of the American public when the show premiered. So the series was psychologically associated with two wars, just as Johnny Mandel, the composer who wrote both the score for *The Russians* movie and the fine theme for the TV program was musically associated with two exceptional productions.

When the U.S. ended the Korean War, the result was a political and military stalemate. When the U.S. withdrew from Vietnam, the result was the collapse of our Vietnamese allies. In contrast, *M*A*S*H* ended in triumph. Its final episode on February 28, 1983 was seen by more people than any other single TV program in history. On that eventful series-ending show, the war also ended, the personnel of the 4077th were sent home, and Mandel's very familiar theme was played for the last time in the context of war.

Mission: Impossible Theme

The fast-paced, strongly vibrating theme of the 1966-1973 action series *Mission: Impossible* clearly radiated a sense of urgency. Something was amiss or being threatened on the international scene, and the Impossible Missions Force was being surreptitiously summoned to correct the problem. Using a team of specialists and an amazing array of high-tech devices and techniques, the IMF cleverly and subtly manipulated the situation until all was resolved.

Argentine-born American composer Lalo Schifrin (1932-) who created the *Mission: Impossible* theme, was at his best with emphatic jazz-oriented music. He also used similar style music for two other successful TV series, *The Man from U.N.C.L.E.* (1964-1968) and *Starsky and Hutch* (1975-1979), both in collaboration with others. The *Mission: Impossible* theme, which so effectively conveyed intrigue, sophistication, challenge, and risk, was undoubtedly his best composition. For that single work, Schifrin won two Grammy Awards.

Only a select few are aware that the IMF continued its clandestine activities after the television series disappeared from the airwaves. Most people think that the network simply canceled the program, but this author and a handful of others privileged to have access to the highest-level secrets know that the IMF, for political reasons, used its electronic might to vaporize all telecasts. In 1988, again for political reasons, the exploits of Jim Phelps (now nearing retirement age) and his highly-skilled associates were allowed back in American living rooms for a couple of years, and then disappeared into secrecy once more. It's nonsense like this that starts rumors and legends.

Perry Mason Theme

Television and the movies have experienced numerous courtroom and legal dramas, including the humorous scenes proving the existence of Santa Claus in the 1947 Christmas classic *Miracle on 34th Street*. But in this forest of media jurisprudence, one enormously big organism stands out conspicuously from all the rest. Punctuated by the bulky frame and dominating face and voice of actor Raymond Burr, the long-running *Perry Mason* television series is the superstar of both courtroom and mystery productions.

Aired from 1957 to 1966, revived unsuccessfully with a totally new cast in 1973-1974, and successfully resurrected with a series of good television movies starting in 1985, *Perry Mason* is an unmatched American cultural institution. (Even before TV, Erle Stanley Gardner's character had been made famous by a batch of best-selling books and a 1943-1955 radio program.)

Three elements have remained constant in the television history of *Perry Mason*. When Raymond Burr portrayed the lawyer who always ultimately won his cases, the show was definitely a success. Even with an almost 20-year gap between the original series and the later television movies, Burr managed to again make his name and Mason's almost synonymous. Burr had several other significant roles, including, ironically, the murderer in Alfred Hitchcock's 1954 thriller *Rear Window*, but he will always be primarily connected with Mason.

The second constant element is Barbara Hale's portrayal of Mason's perpetual associate Della Street in the original series and in the television movies, because she substantially contributed to the flourishing of the show and the movies. Again, like Burr, she will be remembered mostly for her role as Mason's right hand and companion.

The third element is the theme music. Written by otherwise little-known Fred Steiner, the challenging and pulsating composition was always present when *Perry Mason* was on the tube, whether successfully or otherwise. Steiner's theme lent additional strong character to an already strong series, and stamped the Mason sagas with a clear and easily identifiable musical personality. The series probably would have done well with another theme, but Steiner's superlative music surely transported the show to an even higher plateau. Arguably, the "Perry Mason Theme" is the best television theme ever composed, with good challenges by the themes from *Dragnet* and *Mission: Impossible.*

Yet in contrast to Burr and Hale, Steiner's recognition by the public was not appreciably enhanced by the magic of Mason. Ironically, even the perpetual loser, District Attorney Hamilton Berger, has received much more attention. Is that justice?

Peter Gunn Theme

Even if you had never seen a single episode of the 1958-1961 series *Peter Gunn*, you may well have been able to guess from the title that it was a detective show. A polished, sophisticated yet tough private eye, Gunn was one of the best television sleuths of his period.

However, the outstanding feature of the program was not the acting or the plots, but the excellent jazz score. In spite of the merits of the series, the striking music from *Peter Gunn* will probably be remembered long after the show itself has been more or less forgotten. The main theme, in the same dramatic, virile, and rugged style as the scripts, plus the rest of the music, were by the celebrated popular composer Henry Mancini (1924-). With such a success in this brash and impertinent mode of composition, one might presume that this was typical Mancini. Yet his many other songs indicate a general trend to the opposite emotional pole, toward the sweet and melancholy.

The theme for the various *Pink Panther* movies (1964 on) is in a light way somewhat similar to the *Peter Gunn* theme. But the theme for the short-lived television program *Mr. Lucky* (1959-1960) and the well-known songs "Charade" (1963), "Moon River" (1961), and "Days of Wine and Roses" (1962) strongly suggest gentler and more reflective moods. Mancini showed the scope of his talent by very effectively carrying out the varying musical challenges of a suave, resilient detective, an incompetent, bumbling policeman, a slick owner of a gambling boat, the pleasurable times of romance, and a chronically inebriated couple. Note that this essay has touched upon the perpetual social issue of Gunn versus bubbles.

Rawhide Theme

One of the most moving and striking themes in television history was the music for the 1959-1966 western series *Rawhide*. The continuing plot for the very appropriately titled program involved keeping the four-legged critters moving to market on cattle drives and striking fast to keep the dangerous two-legged critters away. (Incidentally, one of the two-legged stars of the series was Clint Eastwood, who became one of the biggest names in Hollywood and Italy because of his leading roles in "spaghetti westerns," *Dirty Harry* dramas, "orangutan" comedies, and other films.)

The rugged theme, with very good words by Ned Washington (1901-1976) and an outstanding melody by the prominent Russian-American composer Dmitri Tiomkin (1894-1979), was effectively belted out by the strong voice of Frankie Laine. Tiomkin was not a novice at creating superlative music for the media. He won no less than three Academy Awards for film scores, *High Noon* (1952), The *High and the Mighty* (1954), and *The Old Man and the Sea* (1958). With so many "highs" in his career (two movies with the word "high" and another involving high water, plus the high volume tones of the *Rawhide* theme), it is not at all surprising that he was at the peak of his profession.

Ned Washington was not exactly an amateur himself. On top of writing the lyrics for "High Noon," "The High and the Mighty," and the *Rawhide* theme, he also wrote the words of another Academy Award-winning song. In collaboration with composer Leigh Harline, he created a totally different style pop classic, "When You Wish Upon a Star," which was introduced in the 1940 Disney animated masterpiece *Pinocchio*. That song, Jimminy Cricket, has been the musical symbol of Walt Disney productions ever since.

Star Trek Theme

Alexander the Great, who made extensive conquests in the fourth century B.C., is a historical symbol of military prowess and courage. The same characteristics apply to the men and women of the starship "Enterprise" who boldly explored and bravely policed the Milky Way galaxy and even beyond. Captain Kirk, Mr. Spock, Dr. McCoy, engineer Scott, and others, as representatives of the Federation, were involved in well-written, imaginative space adventures with an underlying social conscience in the *Star Trek* series from 1966 to 1969.

During its original run, *Star Trek* was not particularly successful and in fact had generally low ratings. After the show was canceled, though, it became a cult phenomenon and the episodes were frequently rerun. Finally, after years of urging by "trekkies," a series of theatrical *Star Trek* movies with most of the original cast were produced beginning in 1979. Although the first movie was somewhat disappointing, subsequent films were much better and helped fuel the fanaticism of *Star Trek* followers. A third stage of the Star Trek story took place in 1987 when another TV series, *Star Trek: The Next Generation*, premiered with a new cast, a new, bigger Enterprise, a new time setting (almost a century later), and with a style reminiscent of the 1960s show.

The excellent, sweeping, dreamlike theme for the original series was written by a man whose name exemplified the strong virtues of the *Star Trek* crew. (He also collaborated on the marchlike theme for *The Next Generation* with Jerry Goldsmith.) How perfect that the musical soul of this science fiction classic was composed by Alexander Courage.

The Twilight Zone Theme

When it comes to science fiction on television, the only mathematical equation is: TV Sci Fi = Twilight Zone. There have been other successful programs with similar purpose and content, but none have attained the legendary status of *The Twilight Zone.* The brainchild of playwright Rod Serling, who was the somber host of the series, *The Twilight Zone*, with its emphasis on the bizarre and offbeat and its many ironies and twists, has become a true television classic.

The program ran from 1959 to 1965, with a short return from 1985 to 1987 after Serling's death. One of the more unusual aspects of this show in which nothing was usual was its theme music. In line with the complex, distorted nature of the plots, there were actually two themes by two different musicians. The most famous one, by French classical composer Marius Constant (1925-), elicited a chaotic and psychotic sensation and matched very well with the psychological setting of the series. The other one, by American composer Bernard Herrmann (1911-1975), also enhanced the eerie mood of the program.

Although Constant was the better-known composer, Herrmann in his own right was a master at creating music for thrillers. At about the same time he also composed the scores for the great Alfred Hitchcock mystery classics *Vertigo* (1958) and *North by Northwest* (1959).

In spite of a wide variety of movie and television music by Herrmann and many works by Constant, the taunting, mocking, dissonant tidbit written by Constant for *The Twilight Zone* is their only composition that is well remembered by the American public. This cultural phenomenon is partly due to the fame of the series, and partly due to the incongruous-sounding theme's major role in making the term "twilight zone" common slang for the fuzzy borderland between reality and fantasy–like this book.

The Untouchables Theme

There were lots of riddles connected with the 1959-1963 television crime series *The Untouchables*. The great popularity of the program was somewhat of a riddle considering its stereotypical, repetitious scripts, the one-dimensional characters, and the severe criticism by critics, public officials, and Italian-American groups. Yet the same characteristics that caused so much controversy– an abundance of bodies riddled with bullets and plots riddled with factual inaccuracies–were probably those that attracted audiences and high ratings. The various protests did not stop the show, and neither did the excess of violence and the excursions into wild historical fantasies that made the real-life figure Eliot Ness and his cadre of prohibition era "Untouchables" into cartoon-like supermen of law enforcement. Eventually, like any fad or novelty, the public just got tired of it as quickly as it had enthusiastically embraced the series when it first appeared.

One more riddle is associated with *The Untouchables* and that was Nelson. The show's dramatic and brash musical theme was written by the successful movie and TV composer Nelson Riddle (1921-), who also created the popular theme for the 1960-1964 series *Route 66* and the score for the somewhat scandalous 1962 movie *Lolita*.

All this is reminiscent of another TV program that followed soon after *The Untouchables*. *Batman* (1966-1968) also had exaggerated characters, lots of crime action, competent guest actors to fill the villain roles, a meteoric rise and a heavy fall, and its "Riddler" character.

But the biggest riddle of all is why you have read this quirky volume almost to the end.

Victory at Sea Theme

Perhaps the greatest documentary in the history of television occurred in its early years. *Victory at Sea*, a 26-episode history of the U.S. Navy and other services in World War II, was broadcast from 1952 to 1953. With outstanding real war footage, intelligent and well-conceived narration, and a brilliant score, *Victory at Sea* was a fitting tribute to the sailors, soldiers, marines, and airmen who participated in the world's most devastating armed conflict.

Richard Rodgers (1902-1979), the illustrious composer of a large number of Broadway musicals, did some of his best work in *Victory at Sea*. Soon after he wrote the music for *South Pacific* (1949) and *The King and I* (1951), both with overseas scenarios, he created the classic-style score that spanned all the oceans. Among the sections were "Guadalcanal March," a brisk testimonial to the men who fought in that bloody battle, and "Beneath the Southern Cross," a smooth tango representing times of diversion and recreation. The latter piece was later turned into the ballad, "No Other Love," in the 1953 musical *Me and Juliet*.

But the battleship of Rodger's music for the documentary was the title theme. Played at the start of each segment, the powerful, ascending and descending theme was photographically complemented by the rising and falling of big ocean swells. On few other occasions has human ingenuity been able to synthesize such a compelling coalescing of sight and sound. The combination of wave and theme in the 1968-1980 police series *Hawaii Five-O* comes close, but it would be hard in any way to match the artistic victory won by the producers of the extraordinary nautical masterpiece of the early 1950s.

The Wild Wild West Theme

Westerns and science fiction stories have for generations been among the most popular types of amusement. The 1965-1970 action series *The Wild Wild West* blended these two genres and produced very entertaining if not always believable programs. James West, an undercover Secret Service Agent during the 1870s, along with his sidekick Artemus Gordon, overcame a succession of sophisticated badmen with brains, brawn, and an amazing array of fantastic devices. Many of the gadgets used, it should be noted, still remain uninvented over a century later. *Wild Wild West* was a strange but successful combination of the style of James Bond with the technology of *Mission: Impossible* at home in the setting of the Old West.

The musical theme of the show, by Richard Markowitz, had a similar multiple personality. In some ways "The Wild Wild West Theme" was as conventional as other themes for westerns, but in other ways it clearly hinted of the unusual. Yet in spite of some tendencies toward nonconformity, it was not nearly as bizarre as the typical science fiction musical motif. Like the show, it effectively mixed the real and the unreal into one of the better TV melodies.

Speaking of real and unreal, this collection of facts and fantasy by an author who was a child in the East and spent his mature years (if any) in the mild, mild Midwest, now ends with *The Wild Wild West*. Please note that this essay on the high-tech TV series, written in a high-tech era, was transacted by very low-tech instruments, paper and pen.

Title Index

Person and Group Index

9781560230298